THE FOOD PROCESSOR FAMILY COOKBOOK

THE
Food
Processor
FAMILY COOKBOOK

120 RECIPES

FOR FAST MEALS MADE FROM SCRATCH

Nicki Sizemore

SONOMA
PRESS

To Ella and Juniper
my adorable and opinionated little eaters

To James
for always eating everything

Contents

Introduction

I hate shredding cheese.

The box grater, in my opinion, is quite possibly the most imperfect tool in the kitchen. It's unstable, it doesn't help me do anything fast, and I've lost a fair bit of knuckle to it. I'm all about cooking foods from scratch, which often requires more prep work than opening a bag, can, or jar, but if my only option were to buy preshredded, bagged (and processed) cheese or use that box grater, I might just be tempted by the bag.

Thank goodness for my food processor! She (yes, it's a she) is a tough gal who can break down a pound of cheese—or carrots or walnuts—in seconds. In the time it would take me to dice half an onion, she finely chops the entire vegetable base for my Bolognese. As a recipe developer and food stylist, cooking is part of my vocation. But when it comes to getting dinner on the table for my family every night, I take any short-cut I can get.

My cooking philosophy can be summed up in seven words: Start from scratch, but keep it simple. There are many gadgets and appliances you can buy for the kitchen, but if you want to cook nutritious, wholesome food for your family, the food processor is the only one you need. It's the tool I turn to more often than any other, whether for prepping the ingredients for tonight's pasta, mixing up granola bars for my five-year-old, puréeing baby food for my nine-month-old, or making my husband's favorite marinated chicken wings. I make my grandma's famous banana bread and even my Thanksgiving pumpkin pie in the processor, too. She isn't the most attractive appliance in the kitchen (I'm looking at you, Mrs. Stand Mixer, with your shiny chrome base), but the processor gets the job done beautifully.

Just because it's a simple machine doesn't mean it can only make simple food. In these pages, I will show you how to make vibrant, creative, and nutritious meals that should be family favorites for years to come. What you'll see here are time-saving, money-saving, from-scratch recipes (with the help of pantry staples) that appeal to eaters of all stripes—from picky kids (got one), to vegetarians and vegans, to folks with food allergies or restrictions (I can't eat gluten), not to mention food lovers looking for delicious meals.

Think of your food processor as your sturdy little friend: Always there for you in a pinch, and always willing to help with the grunt work—including shredding that cheese.

Part One

From Scratch Fast

Let me introduce you to Betty, my friend, my food processor. I couldn't survive without Betty. Let's face it, we live *busy* lives. We don't always have hours—or even *one* hour—to spend cooking. It's no wonder processed foods have taken over our pantries and plates. But this has been at a cost, compromising both nutrition and flavor. It's time to get back into the kitchen, and we need all the help we can get. The food processor is just the friend to turn to. It can cut back prep time and streamline recipes for quicker, more efficient, *and* more delicious results.

1

The Family Processor

I'm assuming you own a food processor. Your friends probably do, too. But how did this appliance end up on our counters? More importantly, how can we take better advantage of a food processor to streamline our time in the kitchen? In this chapter, I'll take you on a brief stroll through its history, and then I'll share tips and techniques for getting the most out of your machine.

From Restaurant Kitchens to the Modern Family's Best Friend

It all started with a robot. Okay; not really. The food processor as we know it, originally called the Robot Coupe (as in *robo-cou*, as opposed to robot cop, which sounds much more exciting), was developed by Frenchman Pierre Verdon, a salesman for a catering company. Realizing that his chef clients were spending an excessive amount of time on food prep—chopping vegetables, pulverizing pâtés, straining purées, and mixing doughs—he developed a solution: a wide machine with a blade in its base that could chop, purée, and knead. The Robot Coupe was introduced in the 1960s in France, and after its success in restaurants, a home version was released in the early 1970s. American engineer Carl Sontheimer refined Verdon's home model, debuting the Cuisinart in the United States in 1973.

By the late '70s, hundreds of thousands of food processors were being sold. Julia Child and James Beard were early advocates, and Beard even wrote a book called *New Recipes for the Cuisinart Food Processor* in 1976. If your mother or grandmother owned a processor at that time, she might have been making those types of recipes, including pâté brisée (pie dough), deviled ham, cheese puffs, and cabbage custard (not two words I usually say together). Chances are, these were special-occasion dishes, and she would lug out her processor only a couple of times a year.

Fast forward to today. While the basic design of the food processor hasn't changed much since the '70s, and although newer models feature more bells and whistles, such as discs and attachments, it has shifted from a special-occasion–only appliance to an everyday workhorse. It has become indispensible for whole and raw food diets, as well as whipping up nutritious vegetable- and herb-based sauces and soups, vegetarian and vegan main dishes, gluten-free flour blends, and quick desserts. Through its ability to cut prep time, today's food processor can help home cooks get fresh, unprocessed foods on the table fast. At least, that's what I'm out to convince you. But first we have to do some rearranging.

Clear a Spot on the Counter

Last year I bought a dress that I was really excited about. It was the type of thing I could throw on to pick up my daughter from school or dress up for a date night. When I got home from the store, I stuck it in my closet, still in its plastic hanging bag. Well guess what? I forgot all about that dress. A whole *year* went by, and I didn't wear it once.

Now, here's the real question: When's the last time you used your food processor? Is it stuffed in a cabinet with all those loose pot lids that fall on your toes every time you pull it out (as mine once was)? First things first: If it's not accessible, your food processor isn't going to get used.

Do what you can to carve out an 8-by-10-inch space on your countertop, or even on an open shelf at arm's height (Betty might be strong, but she ain't light) for your new—or long lost—buddy. Having lived in New York City for five years, I understand that your counter space might be limited. Put the fruit in a hanging basket, stuff the spices in a cabinet, or hang the cooking utensils on the wall, whatever you can do to find a new home for your processor. If it's ready and waiting for you, I promise that you will use it.

Once your processor has its new home, it's time to put it to work. Here's how it can help you get from-scratch meals on the table, often in under an hour.

DITCH THE PROCESSED STUFF Making your own condiments, sauces, and dressings will not only save you hard-earned cash, but you'll end up with more flavorful and nutritious versions of your favorites.

TREAT IT LIKE YOUR SOUS CHEF Cut your dinner prep in half by having the processor do the chopping, slicing, and shredding for you.

GET YOUR SOUP (AND SALAD) ON You're a pulse away from healthy soups like gazpacho, creamy carrot, and roasted vegetable as well as fresh slaws and salads.

BATTER'S UP! Whip up batters for muffins, scones, breads, and doughs in less time, using half the mixing bowls.

DO DESSERT (EVEN ON A WEDNESDAY) From nutritious nut bars and banana ice cream to the easiest (and best ever) chocolate sauce, dessert is only minutes away.

WHEN TO PROCESS AND WHEN TO BLEND

You might be thinking, "Why can't I just use my blender?" While there's a bit of overlap between the functionality of both appliances—for instance, they can both purée a soup or a dressing—the food processor is much more versatile. Since it doesn't require liquid to move the food around the blade like a blender does, a food processor is able to buzz up vegetable purées, dips, spreads, and herb- or vegetable-based sauces, all of which are too thick to process in a regular blender. In addition, since a food processor uses interchangeable blades and discs, it can also handle food prep, including shredding, slicing, kneading, and chopping. Save the blender for smoothies, shakes, nut milks, and liquid-based sauces, and use your food processor for everything else, including:

FOOD PREP chopping vegetables, herbs, meats, nuts, and chocolate; slicing vegetables and hard sausages; shredding vegetables and cheeses; mixing batters

DIPS, SPREADS & NUT BUTTERS whizzing together dips, salsas, and homemade nut butters

HERB- & VEGETABLE-BASED SAUCES pulverizing pestos, chutneys, and no-cook sauces

VEGETABLE PURÉES puréeing vegetables for side dishes or for homemade baby food

DOUGH MAKING pie dough and kneading bread dough

Cups and Bowls and Blades, Oh My

Let's talk nuts and bolts. Chances are you're somewhat familiar with how your food processor works. Maybe you have a bunch of discs and blades somewhere collecting dust. Well, I have good news: You can ditch most of them. We're going to pare things down to the essentials, all of which are easy to use.

Sizes

I own a 14-cup, or what I refer to as a standard-size, processor as well as a mini 3-cup processor. Both are essential in my kitchen, and I use both throughout the book, noting wherever I use a mini.

STANDARD An 11- to 14-cup processor can handle purées, sauces, pestos, soups, and spreads. In addition, this size will do most of the prep work, such as slicing, shredding, chopping, and kneading. There are also 8-cup models on the market, but they're like the goldilocks of food processors—too small for many jobs and too big for the smaller tasks. However, if you've got one, don't stress—you can always process in batches.

MINI A 3- to 4-cup processor is perfect for dressings, condiments, and smaller batches of sauces. It also works great for chopping herbs, garlic, and small quantities of vegetables. They often come with blades only and no disc attachments.

NESTED BOWL PROCESSORS Several models now come with nested work bowls, with both small and large blades. This is like having a standard-size and a mini processor in one, but the drawback is that they often have a lot of parts.

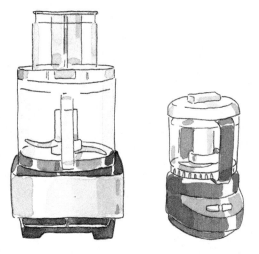

Parts

While some processors now come with a million parts, these are the only ones you need to concern yourself with for the recipes in this book.

WORK BOWL Sometimes referred to as the prep bowl, this is where the magic happens.

LID OR COVER The lid has to be latched in place for the motor to run. Most standard-size models have a large feed tube in the lid that holds the pushers. Mini models have either a feed tube, like in the standard-size, or two small holes in the top of the lid through which oil or liquid can be added.

SMALL AND LARGE PUSHERS OR PLUNGERS These are the parts that fit inside the large feed tube on standard models. Ingredients can be arranged in the large feed tube, then pressed down with the large pusher while the motor is running to shred or slice. The large pusher typically contains a small round feed tube into which liquid can be poured and slim vegetables such as garlic and carrots can be added.

METAL S BLADE This is the sharp metal blade used for chopping and mixing. Most models also come with a plastic dough blade, but I've found that the metal blade works just as well as, if not better than, the dough blade.

SHREDDING DISC This metal disc shreds vegetables and cheese and also works well for grating chocolate and nuts.

SLICING DISC This metal disc thinly slices vegetables, fruits, and hard sausages into thin planks. The slicer is typically 4 mm.

DETACHABLE STEM This attaches the discs to the processor base.

s blade

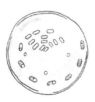

shredding disc

slicing disc

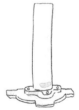

detachable stem

PROCESS VS. PULSE

Food processors typically have either two or three buttons or switches: on and off-pulse, or on, off, and pulse. Some models also have multiple speeds or additional buttons, such as slice/shred and purée/mix. For the recipes in this book, you'll just need the *on* and *pulse* functions, using *on* to process and *pulse* to, well, pulse. Here's what I mean.

PROCESS To process is to turn the machine on and let her rip. This could be for just a few seconds or for up to several minutes. Processing is typically used to finely chop aromatics such as garlic and herbs, to make pastes and purées, or to knead doughs.

PULSE To pulse is to press the pulse button for 1 second, just long enough for you to say "one-one thousand." Pulsing is typically used to chop food without turning it into a purée, to incorporate ingredients, or to mix batters and doughs without overworking them.

Don't Fear the Cleanup

The number-one complaint that I hear from people about why they don't use their processor is that it's a pain to clean. I get it—it can seem like a bear to wash. That's why I have my husband do the dishes. (Really, he's a great dishwasher.) But honestly, with a few tips, the food processor is no harder to clean than a set of bowls and a chef's knife. Here are my top five tips for easier cleanup:

KEEP IT ACCESSIBLE I know we already covered this, but it's *really* important. If you don't have to schlep the processor around, cleanup becomes much more manageable. You're dealing with basically three parts: blade or disk, work bowl, and lid with a pusher.

SCRAPE THE BLADE . . . OR NOT You have two options for de-gunking the blade. First, you can scrape off most of the food with a rubber spatula. Don't go nuts trying to get every last morsel. That's why we have sinks. If you want to skip that step, scrape most of the food out of the work bowl, leaving the blade inside. Reassemble the processor with the still-dirty blade, and pulse a few times. All the food on the blade will be flung to the sides of the work bowl, leaving you with a wiped-clean blade.

USE A SCRUB BRUSH The easiest way to wash the blade is with a long-handled scrub brush, as sponges tend to get stuck on the edges. Soap it up and scrub just like you would a knife, holding on to the plastic portion. A scrub brush is also great for cleaning the feed tube in the lid.

USE THE DISHWASHER If you've got one, go for it. Most work bowls and lids can go in the dishwasher, although some mini processor bowls must only go on the top shelf to prevent warping, so be sure to check your manual. However—and this is important— never put the metal blade and discs in the dishwasher, as it can dull the edges.

WASH RIGHT AWAY OR SOAK This is the most important tip I can offer you. After you use the food processor, wash it right away or fill it with soapy water and let it soak. That way, the food inside will wipe right out, instead of hardening and becoming annoying to scrub later—a universal truth for any kitchen tool. I think it's easiest to wash the bowl and blade immediately. It only takes a minute or two, and that way I'm not left with additional cleanup after we eat. But I'm also a type A, so there's that.

Safety Reminders

Food processors are typically very safe to use—unlike, say, the mandoline, which my husband has renamed the "tool of death"—but there are a few things to keep in mind.

HANDLING Hold the blade by its plastic stem and the discs by their edges. Always use the pusher to guide food through the feed tube. Those shredding and slicing discs are no joke. When you're emptying the work bowl, either remove the blade first or hold it in place with your finger or a spatula so that it doesn't come tumbling out. Some models even have a blade lock system.

LID REMOVAL Always wait until the blade and discs stop moving before removing the lid.

STORAGE When it comes to storing your processor and its parts, don't do as I did and pile all your discs and blades in the back of a cabinet, so that when you absentmindedly reach in there one day, you end up stabbing yourself with the metal blade. Bad idea. Store the work bowl on the base with the blade inside. Keep the discs in a storage container. And, as always, keep the sharp stuff away from children.

EVERYTHING ELSE Read your manual. Some appliance manuals could go right in the recycling bin and you'd never miss them. This isn't one of those.

Okay. Now that we've covered safety, let's get to the good stuff: food.

Processor Pro: Making Your Own Recipes—Faster

While I wish I had hours to spend in the kitchen every day, the reality is that I'm usually racing to get dinner on the table in that all-too-fleeting time after work and before the kids' baths (or impending meltdowns). Once I started thinking of my food processor as my sous chef, however—there to do the chopping, slicing, and grating for me—I realized I could cut my prep time in half. The cheese for the homemade macaroni can be shredded in less than a minute, as opposed to the five minutes or so I would typically spend cursing my box grater, and the vegetables for the curry can be chopped in seconds. I can even whip up a quick homemade banana or mango "ice cream" after dinner in mere seconds, which, I can't lie, kind of makes me feel like a superhero.

Once you let your food processor become part of your everyday routine, you'll be able to use it to streamline your own favorite recipes. If you're making a soup or stew with a lot of vegetables as the base, consider pulsing them in the food processor to chop. If a recipe calls for a mess of minced garlic, shallots, or herbs, let the mini processor do it for you—just toss them in whole, and process until minced. Even batters for muffins, quick breads, and cakes can be made in the food processor without dirtying any bowls. The trick is to purée the wet ingredients first, then sprinkle the dry ingredients evenly over the top and pulse just until the flour is mostly incorporated. A quick swipe with a spatula, and your batter is ready to bake. Below are a few of my family's longtime favorite recipes, and how I adapted them using my processor.

MARINARA SAUCE (PAGE 42) Homemade marinara usually takes over an hour to prepare. With the food processor, it comes together in half the time, with half the work. I throw the vegetables into the processor and pulse until finely chopped. This does double duty—the finely chopped veggies then cook twice as fast.

POTATO GRATIN (PAGE 114) The shredding disc shreds the cheese in seconds, then—without washing the work bowl—the slicing disc perfectly slices the potatoes. That means I can make a gratin even on a weeknight. I use the same technique with other root vegetables, such as sweet potatoes and winter squash.

GRANDMA'S BANANA BREAD (PAGE 84) Making banana bread involves several steps when done by hand, from puréeing the bananas, to mixing the dry and wet ingredients in separate bowls, to folding them together. With the processor, I purée the bananas first, then process the wet ingredients until smooth, and finish by sprinkling the dry ingredients over the top and pulsing just to incorporate.

THE BEST FOODS FOR FIRST FOODS

My oldest daughter was born the year we had our first garden surplus. I started making her baby food pretty much as a way to use up the glut of kale and squash. I'd steam and purée the veggies, then freeze them in silicone trays. Five years later, now that I have my second daughter, my approach has become even more relaxed: I simply purée her portions of whatever we're eating for dinner.

Making your own baby food saves you a ton of money, exposes your children to a world of interesting flavors that they couldn't get out of a jar, and puts you in control of what goes into their bodies (and what doesn't—no additives, chemicals, or sweeteners here). The food processor is indispensible when it comes to making baby food from scratch. If you're embarking on this journey (and it's a fun one, I promise!), here are a few tips before you get started.

FORGET RICE CEREAL Prepackaged rice and grain cereals are highly processed and refined. Tests conducted in 2012 by Consumer Reports even found worrisome levels of arsenic in rice products, including baby cereals, some of which were revealed to have levels of arsenic at levels five times higher than those found in other grains, such as oatmeal. Instead, start with pureed vegetables and fruits, such as avocados, bananas, spinach, peaches, and apples.

START SMOOTH Start with smooth purées, which are easier for young babies to swallow, adding water or breast milk/formula to thin if needed. As your baby grows and becomes a more experienced eater, you can start to incorporate texture.

USE HERBS AND SPICES Don't be afraid to flavor your baby's food! Remember, you're helping to develop adventurous palates. Throw some curry powder into the squash, add a touch of cinnamon to the apples, or add fresh thyme to the beets.

FREEZE PURÉES Freeze purées in silicone ice cube or baby food trays. Once frozen, store the cubes in labeled zip-top bags in the freezer. That way you'll always have a stash of nutritious, homemade food on hand.

STAY AWAY FROM HONEY Don't give your infant honey during the first year of life, as it may contain bacteria that can lead to infant botulism.

Baby Food Chart

FOOD	PREP AND PROCESSING INSTRUCTIONS	SUGGESTED FLAVORINGS (choose 1 or 2 to add before processing)
Apple	Peel and core apples. Coarsely chop and simmer with a few splashes of water until very soft. Transfer to the food processor, and process to desired consistency.	Ground cinnamon Ground nutmeg
Asparagus	Discard woody ends of asparagus and coarsely chop. Steam until tender. Transfer to the food processor and process until smooth, adding a few splashes of the steaming liquid to thin, if needed.	Chopped fresh chives Chopped fresh parsley Chopped fresh tarragon
Avocado	Halve avocados, and discard the seed. Scoop the flesh into the food processor, and process to desired consistency, adding breast milk, formula, or water to thin, if needed.	Chopped fresh cilantro Ground cumin
Banana	Peel bananas and add to the food processor. Process to desired consistency, adding breast milk, formula, or water to thin, if needed.	Ground cardamom Ground cinnamon
Beet	Boil or steam whole beets until very tender. Peel and coarsely chop. Transfer to the food processor, and process to desired consistency, adding a few splashes of the cooking liquid to thin, if needed.	Chopped fresh tarragon Chopped fresh thyme
Blueberry	Simmer blueberries with a few splashes of water until they release their juices and are very tender. Transfer to the food processor, and process to desired consistency.	Ground cardamom Ground cinnamon Ground nutmeg
Broccoli or Cauliflower	Cut broccoli or cauliflower into florets, and steam until tender. Transfer to the food processor with a few splashes of the steaming liquid. Process to desired consistency, adding additional liquid if needed.	Cooked apples or pears Garam masala Leeks

Baby Food Chart

FOOD	PREP AND PROCESSING INSTRUCTIONS	SUGGESTED FLAVORINGS (choose 1 or 2 to add before processing)
Butternut Squash	Halve the squash lengthwise, and discard the seeds. Bake cut-side down on parchment-lined baking sheet in 400°F oven until very tender, about 50 minutes. Scoop the flesh into the food processor, and process to desired consistency, adding water or broth to thin, if needed.	Ground cinnamon Ground cloves Curry powder
Carrot	Trim, peel, and coarsely chop carrots. Steam until very tender. Transfer to the food processor with a few splashes of the steaming liquid. Process to desired consistency, adding additional liquid if needed.	Chopped fresh mint Ground nutmeg
Fish	Break up fillets of cooked white fish, such as wild flounder or cod, into the food processor, being careful that all bones are removed, and process with stock or water to desired consistency.	Chopped fresh thyme Cooked vegetables
Meat	Transfer chopped, cooked chicken, beef, or lamb to the food processor, and process with a few splashes of broth or water to desired consistency.	Chopped fresh rosemary Cooked vegetables
Pea	Boil or steam peas until bright green and tender. Transfer to the food processor with a few splashes of the cooking liquid. Process to desired consistency, adding additional liquid if needed.	Chopped fresh mint
Peach	Peel peaches with a serrated vegetable peeler, then halve them and discard the pits. Coarsely chop the peaches, and simmer with a few splashes of water until very soft. Transfer to the food processor, and process to desired consistency.	Ground cardamom Ground nutmeg Chopped fresh thyme
Pear	Peel and core pears. Coarsely chop and simmer with a few splashes of water until very soft. Transfer to the food processor, and process to desired consistency.	Ground cinnamon Ground cloves Ground nutmeg

continued

Baby Food Chart

FOOD	PREP AND PROCESSING INSTRUCTIONS	SUGGESTED FLAVORINGS (choose 1 or 2 to add before processing)
Prune	Coarsely chop pitted prunes. Simmer with a few splashes of water until very tender. Transfer to the food processor, and process to desired consistency.	Ground cloves Chopped fresh thyme
Red Lentil	Rinse red lentils and soak in water for 30 minutes. Drain and transfer to a saucepan with two parts water to one part lentils. Bring to a boil, then reduce to a simmer and cook until the lentils are falling apart and tender, about 30 minutes. Transfer to the food processor, and process to desired consistency.	Ground cumin Curry powder
Root Vegetable	Peel and chop assorted root vegetables, such as carrots, celery root, parsnips, sweet potatoes, and squash. Toss with olive oil, and roast in a 400°F oven until very tender, about 45 minutes. Transfer to the food processor with a splash of water or broth, and process to desired consistency, adding additional liquid to thin, if needed.	Chopped fresh rosemary Chopped fresh sage
Spinach or Swiss Chard	Steam greens until wilted and tender. Transfer to the food processor, and process to desired consistency, adding a splash of the steaming liquid to thin, if needed.	Chopped fresh basil Chopped fresh chives
String Bean	Trim green or yellow wax beans. Steam or boil until very tender. Transfer to the food processor with a few splashes of the cooking liquid, and process to desired consistency, adding additional liquid if needed.	Chopped fresh basil Chopped fresh mint
Sweet Potato	Peel and chop sweet potatoes. Steam until soft. Transfer to the food processor with a few splashes of the steaming liquid. Process to desired consistency, adding additional liquid if needed.	Ground cinnamon

What's Next?

Now that we've completed Food Processor 101 (you did great!), it's almost time to get cooking. Before we hop in, I'm going to share some of my favorite kitchen pointers, including a list of must-have kitchen equipment. These tools (don't worry; there aren't many) will enable you to tackle nearly any recipe under the sun.

I'll also share my favorite pantry staples. With the help of these standbys, it's possible to whip up dinner even when the fridge is nearly empty. And finally, I'll divulge insider tips for making the most of your food processor. Here we go!

In the Kitchen

Welcome to my kitchen. It's by far our favorite room in the house, where we eat, talk, do homework, and, of course, cook. In this chapter I'll show you around, first guiding you through the few kitchen tools I couldn't live without, then giving you a peek inside my pantry (I can't promise it's clean). I'll also share some of my favorite food processor tips and tricks, helping you use your machine to its best capability, as well as ensuring it will last a lifetime.

Supporting Equipment

While the food processor is certainly a wonder woman, she still needs the support of other basic tools in the kitchen. In addition to the standards—a good set of sharp knives, mixing bowls, liquid and dry measuring cups, measuring spoons, whisks, wooden spoons, and rubber spatulas—these are my must-have essentials:

FINE-MESH STRAINERS A small strainer with a handle is perfect for draining cans of beans and straining soups. A large strainer with a base is essential for draining pasta or blanched vegetables.

FISH SPATULA I use this almost exclusively for flipping not only fish, but also burgers, vegetable cakes, and pancakes.

HONING STEEL If you've ever tried to slice a tomato but your knife wouldn't budge through the skin, it needs to be honed. Running your knife along a honing steel at a slight angle realigns the edge, keeping it razor sharp.

MICROPLANE Nothing works better for zesting lemons, finely grating cheese or chocolate, or grating garlic and ginger into a paste.

HOW TO HONE A KNIFE WITHOUT A HONING STEEL

No matter how crazy it sounds, sharp knives are indeed safer and easier to use than dull ones. A dull knife requires more pressure—read: work—to chop through food, therefore creating a greater likelihood of the blade slipping and causing injury (been there, done that!).

While I consider a honing steel a kitchen essential, if you don't have one, here's a cool work-around I learned while working with *Fine Cooking* magazine. Find a ceramic mug with a flat, unglazed ring on the bottom. Run both sides of your knife along the ring at a 45-degree angle. This will realign the edge, giving you a nice, sharp blade. It's not a good long-term solution, however, so I still recommend getting yourself a honing steel.

POTS AND PANS A 12-inch regular and a 12-inch nonstick heavy-bottomed skillet with at least 1 lid are the workhorses of the kitchen. A small (1 to 2 quart), a medium (3 to 4 quart), and a large (10 to 12 quart) saucepan are enough to handle any task, from melting butter, to cooking rice, to boiling a pound of pasta.

SPIDER These wide, wire mesh skimmers make it super easy to pull vegetables and pasta out of boiling water, or to pull falafel and fries out of hot oil.

TONGS Tongs are the ultimate multitaskers, perfect for browning meat, tossing pasta, and serving salads.

Pantry Staples

With a well-stocked pantry of essentials, it's possible to throw a meal together even when the refrigerator is nearly bare. These are my sidekicks, the Robin to my Batman, the everyday pantry staples that I couldn't live without:

BAKING POWDER AND BAKING SODA for baked goods

BEANS, CANNED for soups, salads, side dishes, and tacos

CHOCOLATE for baked goods, desserts, and snacks

COCONUT MILK, CANNED for dressings, sauces, curries, soups, smoothies, and desserts

FLOUR for baked goods, breads, and pizza, including all-purpose, gluten-free, and whole-wheat flours

FRUIT, FROZEN for smoothies and desserts

MUSTARD, DIJON for dressings, marinades, sauces, and sandwiches

NUTS AND SEEDS for snacks, salads, breakfasts, and baked goods

OIL, EXTRA-VIRGIN COCONUT for sautéing, as well as for baked goods

OIL, EXTRA-VIRGIN OLIVE for sautéing, as well as for dressings and marinades

OIL, GRAPESEED OR CANOLA for sautéing, frying, grilling, and stir-frying, as well as for dressings and marinades

PASTA/DRIED NOODLES for pastas, soups, and salads

PEAS, FROZEN for salads, side dishes, and soups

SPICES for soups, sautés, side dishes, dressings, baked goods, and desserts. My spice rack includes everything from black pepper and kosher salt to ground cardamom and chili powder. Note: I use kosher salt most often for consistency, but I also use a variety of sea salts, particularly for garnish.

SRIRACHA AND HOT SAUCE for dressings, sauces, marinades, and stir-fries

SWEETENERS for baked goods, desserts, breakfasts, dressings, and marinades. My top three include honey, maple syrup, and sugar.

TAMARI OR SOY SAUCE for dressings, sauces, marinades, and stir-fries. Tamari is a Japanese soy sauce that typically contains little to no wheat. If you do not eat gluten, make sure you purchase tamari that's labeled wheat-free or gluten-free.

TOMATOES, CANNED for pasta sauces, soups, stews, and braises

VINEGARS for dressings, marinades, and sauces, including apple cider, balsamic, red wine, rice wine, and white wine

WHOLE GRAINS for salads, side dishes, breakfasts, and baked goods, including quinoa, rice, rolled oats, and more

Never-Never Land

If you've invested in a food processor, you know they're not cheap. However, if you take care of it, it can last you a lifetime. To keep your machine running smoothly for years to come, as well as to keep yourself safe in the process, there are just a few things you'll want to steer clear of.

Never

PUT THE BLADE IN THE DISHWASHER I never put my good knives in the dishwasher, as it wears down the edges. Similarly, I never put the food processor blades and discs in the dishwasher. Washing them by hand will ensure they'll stay sharp for years to come.

OVERFILL THE WORK BOWL WITH HOT LIQUID OR SOUP If you overfill the work bowl before processing, the mixture can leak out of the sides and the lid, which could get dangerous if dealing with hot liquids. Fill the work bowl only a third to halfway up the sides when puréeing hot soups. I also place a dish towel over the top to prevent splatters.

PROCESS HARD FOODS THAT YOU COULDN'T CUT WITH A KNIFE If your knife can't cut it, the blade shouldn't either. Not that I expect you'll be processing chicken bones or your kids' marbles anytime soon.

GRIND WHOLE SPICES Along the same lines as above, whole spices are too hard to process in the food processor and can end up scratching the sides, leaving you with a cloudy work bowl. Save whole spices for a coffee grinder.

Tips for Making the Most Out of Your Processor

Over the years, I've picked up several tricks and tips to help me make the most out of my gal Betty—er, my food processor.

Chopping

To finely chop small aromatics such as garlic and chiles, drop them through the small round feed tube while the food processor motor is running—the spinning blade will chop them evenly.

To finely chop larger vegetables such as onions, carrots, and celery, cut them into similar-size 1- to 2-inch pieces, then pulse them in the food processor until finely chopped. This will ensure that they chop evenly without turning into a paste.

To finely chop meat or fish for burgers, meatballs, or sausages, cut the meat into ½- to 1-inch cubes and freeze them for 10 to 20 minutes, until hardened along the edges. Then pulse the meat in the food processor until finely chopped. This will ensure that the meat will chop evenly, without turning into a paste.

Slicing and Shredding

When slicing or shredding, arrange the ingredients in an even layer in the large feed tube, being careful not to exceed the max fill line. I spent years cutting food to fit within the small round feed tube, not realizing that I could remove the large pusher, load in a bigger quantity of food (large potato chunks, a block of cheese), then press it all down at once. Typically the machine needs to be turned on, but the motor won't start running until the pusher clicks down on the latch.

When shredding cheese, stick with hard cheeses such as Parmesan, Cheddar, and Gruyère. The cheeses need to be cold before shredding—either add them straight out of the fridge or freeze them for 5 to 10 minutes before shredding. Don't shred soft cheeses such as mozzarella, as they'll turn to mush.

CONSIDERING ORGANICS

We're lucky to have an awesome farmers' market in our town, where we buy a large portion of our vegetables, fruits, meat, and eggs. Produce that's grown locally and in season is not only much more delicious (case in point: August vs. January tomatoes), but it's also more nutritious and usually more economical.

I try to buy organic ingredients as much as possible. They're grown without the use of synthetic pesticides, chemicals, antibiotics, or growth hormones. This is particularly important since I'm feeding two small girls, including a baby. However, my motto is that if I can't find it, I don't sweat it, and if it's too expensive, then I forget it. If I can't find what I need, or if it's too costly to buy organic, I refer to the Dirty Dozen and Clean Fifteen lists (page 242) to decide what to avoid or splurge on.

Puréeing and Mixing

When puréeing foods, be sure to scrape down the sides every now and then. If the mixture ends up along the sides of the work bowl without smoothing out into a purée, additional ingredients or liquids need to be added.

When mixing batters, it's important not to overprocess. First purée the wet ingredients, then pulse in the dry ingredients until just incorporated. Stir in any remaining streaks of flour using a rubber spatula.

This Book's Recipes

Each recipe in this book will guide you, step-by-step, in how to use the food processor to maximize deliciousness and minimize your time in the kitchen, specifying which blade or discs to use and when, as well as which size processor to use. Unless noted, you can assume that it's a standard-size processor.

In the following pages, you'll find recipes that will please every palate and preference, from kid-friendly to vegetarian, vegan, gluten-free, or nut-free, along with party-friendly appetizers, sauces, side dishes, and main courses. These are vibrant, nourishing dishes that reflect my belief that eating healthy means enjoying a colorful variety of whole, unprocessed foods. I also live by the motto "Everything in moderation, including moderation," so there are also plenty of delectable desserts to finish things off. Strap on your apron, and let's get cooking. I'll bring the wine.

Part Two
Recipes for the Kitchen

From the best roasted tomato sauce, to homemade mayonnaise and ketchup, to flaky pie crusts, and a pizza dough that can be whipped up on a weeknight, the food processor is the ultimate tool for making quick, from-scratch sauces, condiments, dips, and doughs. Many people think of sauces as a supporting element in a meal, but I believe they're essential. The recipes you'll find here will flavor and make memorable your proteins, vegetables, and starches. Some children don't love veggies, but if you offer an unbelievable hummus or buttermilk-herb dressing on the side, watch them put away their carrots, celery, and snap peas. If you've been buying jarred pesto or salsa for some time, you're about to taste just how vibrant an easy homemade version can be, transforming the average pasta or fish dish into a weeknight treat. So plug in your processor, and let's get started!

Sauces, Dressings & Seasonings

Pesto

Prep time: 10 minutes

GLUTEN-FREE, VEGETARIAN

Everybody needs a quick pesto recipe. It can transform even the most humdrum of dishes, from pizzas and pastas to burgers, grilled meats, roasted fish, simple sandwiches, and platters of vegetables, into a culinary experience. Although I tested the measurements here, pesto is incredibly forgiving, so feel free to just eyeball everything. You can also customize it to make it your own—try switching up the basil with parsley, arugula, or mint or adding hot pepper flakes for some heat. MAKES ABOUT 1 CUP

1 large garlic clove, peeled

2 cups packed fresh basil leaves

¼ cup toasted pine nuts or walnuts
(see How-to, page 37)

½ cup freshly grated Parmigiano-Reggiano or
pecorino romano cheese, or a mix of both

Juice of ½ lemon, or more for seasoning

Salt

Freshly ground black pepper

½ cup extra-virgin olive oil

INGREDIENT INFO Why Parmigiano and not Parmesan? Since there are so few ingredients in a pesto, each one makes a big difference. Italian Parmigiano-Reggiano has an exceptional nutty, sweet, and salty taste that lends big flavor to this pesto. However, if you can't find it, you'll still end up with a delicious sauce using generic Parmesan—just don't use the processed stuff in the green canister, please!

1. Fit the food processor with the *s blade*. With the motor running, drop the garlic clove through the feed tube to finely chop. Stop and scrape down the sides.

2. Add the basil, pine nuts, grated cheese, lemon juice, and a large pinch of salt and pepper. Process until finely chopped. Stop and scrape down the sides.

3. With the motor running, slowly pour the olive oil through the feed tube, stopping halfway to scrape down the sides. Taste and season the pesto with additional salt, pepper, or lemon juice as needed.

STORAGE The pesto can be refrigerated for up to 3 days or frozen in an airtight container or zip-top bag for up to 1 month. Drizzle a bit more olive oil over the top, and place a piece of plastic wrap directly on the surface to prevent it from turning brown. Bring to room temperature before serving.

Vegan Pesto

Prep time: 10 minutes

GLUTEN-FREE, VEGAN

You won't miss the dairy in this vibrant pesto! In place of the cheese, this version has more nuts, which lend a savory flavor and thick texture. If you can find it, nutritional yeast (a deactivated form of yeast that comes in flakes) imparts a rich, savory, cheese-like depth of flavor, although it's not necessary. MAKES ABOUT 1 CUP

1 large garlic clove, peeled

2 cups packed fresh basil leaves

½ cup toasted pine nuts or walnuts (see How-to)

3 tablespoons nutritional yeast (optional)

Juice of ½ lemon, or more for seasoning

Salt

Freshly ground black pepper

½ cup extra-virgin olive oil

HOW-TO To toast pine nuts, walnuts, pecans, cashews, almonds, pumpkin seeds, or even coconut flakes, preheat the oven to 350°F. Spread the nuts, seeds, or flakes on a baking sheet in an even layer, and bake for 10 to 15 minutes. Stir halfway through toasting time to ensure even browning, and check frequently near the end to avoid burning.

1. Fit the food processor with the *s blade*. With the motor running, drop the garlic clove through the feed tube to finely chop. Stop and scrape down the sides.

2. Add the basil, pine nuts, nutritional yeast (if using), lemon juice, and a large pinch of salt and pepper. Process until finely chopped. Stop and scrape down the sides.

3. With the motor running, slowly pour the olive oil through the feed tube, stopping halfway to scrape down the sides. Taste and season the pesto with additional salt, pepper, or lemon juice as needed.

STORAGE The pesto can be refrigerated for up to 3 days or frozen in an airtight container or zip-top bag for up to 1 month. Drizzle a bit more olive oil over the top, and place a piece of plastic wrap directly on the surface to prevent it from turning brown. Bring to room temperature before serving.

Chimichurri Sauce

This bright, zippy sauce is like pairing an emerald necklace with a simple black dress—it instantly adds sparkle. Chimichurri harkens from Argentina, where it's traditionally served with meat. Drizzle it over thinly sliced Marinated Flank Steak with Chimichurri (page 180) or serve it with grilled chicken or fish. Although it's not traditional, I add a touch of honey to the sauce, which lends a subtle hint of sweetness for balance. MAKES 1 CUP

1 large garlic clove, peeled

1½ cups (about 1 large bunch) lightly packed fresh cilantro

1 cup lightly packed fresh parsley

1½ tablespoons red wine vinegar

Juice of ½ lemon

1 teaspoon honey

½ teaspoon dried oregano

¼ to ½ teaspoon red pepper flakes

Kosher salt

Freshly ground black pepper

½ cup extra-virgin olive oil

STORAGE The chimichurri sauce can be refrigerated for up to 1 week or frozen in an airtight container or zip-top bag for up to 1 month. Bring to room temperature before serving.

1. Fit the food processor with the *s blade*. With the motor running, drop the garlic through the feed tube to chop.

2. Add the cilantro, parsley, red wine vinegar, lemon juice, honey, oregano, and red pepper flakes. Season with salt and pepper. Process to a coarse paste, stopping to scrape down the sides occasionally.

3. With the motor running, slowly drizzle in the olive oil. Process until incorporated, stopping to scrape down the sides occasionally. Taste and season with additional salt and pepper as needed.

4. Transfer to a bowl, and let sit at room temperature for 10 minutes to 1 hour to let the flavors meld.

Italian Salsa Verde

Prep time: 10 minutes, plus 10 minutes to sit

GLUTEN-FREE

Whenever I need to escape the everyday, I make this classic Italian "green sauce." It instantly evokes Italy, especially when spooned over Tuscan Grilled Skirt Steak with Salsa Verde (page 182). The sauce is made of herbs, capers, garlic, shallots, and anchovy. Don't be put off by the anchovy—it adds depth of flavor, but you won't taste it. While I could eat this with a spoon, it's also great over grilled white fish, or even tossed with pasta. Buon appetito! MAKES ABOUT ⅔ CUP

1 garlic clove, peeled
½ small shallot
1½ teaspoons drained capers
1 anchovy fillet, rinsed and patted dry
1 teaspoon finely chopped fresh rosemary
1 teaspoon fresh thyme leaves
1 cup lightly packed fresh parsley
1 tablespoon coarsely chopped walnuts
¼ teaspoon red wine vinegar
Kosher salt
Freshly ground black pepper
½ cup extra-virgin olive oil

STORAGE The salsa verde can be refrigerated for 1 week or frozen in an airtight container or zip-top bag for up to 1 month. Bring to room temperature before serving.

1. Fit the mini food processor with the *s blade*. Add the garlic and shallot. Process to finely chop. Stop and scrape down the sides.

2. Add the capers, anchovy, rosemary, thyme, parsley, walnuts, and red wine vinegar, and season with salt and pepper. Process until finely chopped, stopping and scraping down the sides occasionally.

3. With the motor running, drizzle the olive oil through the feed tube or through one of the holes in the lid. Taste and season with additional salt and pepper as needed. Transfer to a bowl, and let sit at room temperature for 10 minutes to 1 hour to let the flavors meld.

Tahini Sauce

Prep time: 5 minutes

GLUTEN-FREE, NUT-FREE, VEGAN

This garlicky, creamy sauce is amazing with Falafel (page 208) as well as drizzled over roasted vegetables or grilled meat kebabs. It's a delicious salad dressing, too—try tossing it with crispy romaine lettuce, chickpeas, cucumbers, tomatoes, and mint. Tahini is a paste made from sesame seeds that have been toasted, hulled, and ground. MAKES ABOUT 1 CUP

2 small garlic cloves, peeled

½ cup well-stirred tahini

3 tablespoons freshly squeezed lemon juice

5 tablespoons water

Kosher salt

3 tablespoons extra-virgin olive oil

STORAGE The tahini sauce can be refrigerated for up to 1 week. Bring to room temperature before serving. The sauce will thicken as it chills, so you might need to add another tablespoon or two of water before serving.

1. Fit the mini food processor with the *s blade*. Add the garlic, and chop. Stop and scrape down the sides.

2. Add the tahini, lemon juice, and water, and season with salt. Process until smooth, stopping and scraping down the sides occasionally.

3. With the motor running, slowly drizzle the olive oil through the feed tube or through one of the holes in the lid. Taste and season with additional salt as needed. If you prefer a thinner sauce, add an additional 1 to 2 tablespoons water.

Roasted Tomato Sauce

Prep time: 10 minutes • Cook time: 25 minutes

GLUTEN-FREE, NUT-FREE, VEGAN

This has got to be the easiest fresh tomato sauce ever, and the flavor is phenomenal—pure and bright. Plum tomatoes get roasted until slightly caramelized and sweet, then processed until smooth with a bit of basil. It's simplicity at its best. This is our favorite sauce for homemade pizzas (page 75). MAKES ABOUT 3 CUPS

8 to 10 plum tomatoes (about 2 pounds), cored and halved lengthwise

2 tablespoons extra-virgin olive oil

Kosher salt

Freshly ground black pepper

½ teaspoon sugar

2 teaspoons balsamic vinegar

¼ teaspoon freshly squeezed lemon juice

2 tablespoons chopped fresh basil

STORAGE The tomato sauce can be refrigerated for up to 5 days or frozen for up to 3 months.

INGREDIENT INFO Have you ever made a sauce or soup, seasoned it well with salt and pepper, but still felt that something was missing? Chances are it was acid. A touch of acid at the end, such as a few drops of vinegar or lemon juice, will brighten the flavors and put everything in balance.

1. Preheat the oven to 450°F. Line a large baking sheet with foil.

2. Place the tomatoes on the baking sheet. Add the olive oil, and season with salt and pepper. Toss to coat.

3. Arrange the tomatoes in an even layer, cut-side up. Sprinkle the sugar and balsamic evenly over the tomatoes. Roast for 25 minutes, or until the tomatoes are lightly browned on the edges. Don't worry if the foil starts to blacken in spots.

4. Fit the food processor with the *s blade*. Add the tomatoes, and process until smooth. Season with salt and pepper. Add the lemon juice and basil, and pulse to combine. Taste and season with additional salt and pepper as needed.

Quick Marinara Sauce

Prep time: 10 minutes • Cook time: 20 minutes

GLUTEN-FREE, NUT-FREE, VEGETARIAN

Whether serving this marinara over a plate of spaghetti, tossing it with meatballs, layering it into lasagna, or spreading it on pizza, you'll find it's as versatile—and flattering—as your favorite jeans. Marinara typically needs to cook for about an hour, but with the help of the food processor, this version needs only about 10 minutes to simmer. MAKES ABOUT 3¼ CUPS

1 small onion, coarsely chopped

½ medium carrot, coarsely chopped

1 (3-inch) piece celery, coarsely chopped

2 tablespoons extra-virgin olive oil

Kosher salt

Freshly ground black pepper

2 garlic cloves, minced

1 teaspoon minced fresh rosemary

1 teaspoon dried Italian herb mix

2 tablespoons tomato paste

1 (28-ounce) can San Marzano
  crushed tomatoes

Pinch sugar

¼ cup grated Parmesan cheese

1 to 2 tablespoons heavy (whipping) cream

1. Fit the food processor with the *s blade*. Add the onion, carrot, and celery, and pulse until finely chopped.

2. In a medium heavy-bottomed saucepan over medium heat, heat the olive oil. Add the chopped vegetables, and season with salt and pepper. Cook, stirring occasionally, until softened, about 7 minutes.

3. Add the garlic, rosemary, and Italian herb mix. Cook until fragrant, 1 to 2 minutes. Stir in the tomato paste, and cook, stirring, for 1 minute. The bottom of the pan should start to look brown as the tomato paste caramelizes. Pour in the crushed tomatoes, and add the sugar.

4. Bring the mixture to a boil, then reduce it to a lively simmer. Cook, partially covered, for 10 minutes, or until the vegetables are tender, stirring occasionally. Remove the sauce from the heat and let cool slightly.

5. Rinse out and reassemble the food processor. Add the sauce, and process until smooth. Return the sauce to the pot, and add the Parmesan cheese and heavy cream. Season with salt and pepper. Reheat over medium-low heat.

STORAGE The marinara sauce can be refrigerated for up to 1 week.

TIME SAVER I often double the recipe and freeze half of it for quick meals down the line. The trick is to freeze the sauce *before* adding the Parmesan cheese and heavy cream. After you purée the sauce, transfer it to a freezer-safe container or a large zip-top bag. When you're ready to use, simply defrost and add the Parmesan and cream. *Bravissimo!*

Dijon Vinaigrette

Prep time: 5 minutes

GLUTEN-FREE, NUT-FREE, VEGETARIAN

This is my go-to salad dressing, and I almost always have a jar in the fridge. It's vibrant, bright, and perfect with nearly any kind of salad. Toss it with greens, shaved vegetables, or chopped garden goodies. Your vegetables will thank you. MAKES ABOUT 1 CUP

1 large garlic clove, peeled

½ small shallot, peeled and coarsely chopped

1 tablespoon Dijon or whole-grain mustard

2 teaspoons honey

Pinch chopped fresh or dried herbs, such as rosemary, thyme, basil, oregano, or tarragon (optional)

6 tablespoons raw apple cider vinegar or white wine vinegar

Kosher salt

Freshly ground black pepper

½ cup extra-virgin olive oil

HOW-TO When tasting salad dressing, it's best to dip a piece of lettuce into it. That way, you can taste how the dressing will interact with the greens. Sturdy, crunchy lettuces can stand up to more acidic dressings, while tender, delicate greens are best with gentler dressings.

1. Fit the mini food processor with the *s blade*. Add the garlic, shallot, mustard, honey, herbs (if using), and vinegar, and season with salt and pepper. Process until smooth. Stop and scrape down the sides.

2. With the motor running, slowly drizzle the olive oil through the feed tube or through one of the holes in the lid. Taste and season with additional salt and pepper as needed. If you prefer a less tart dressing, add another tablespoon of olive oil and process until combined.

STORAGE The vinaigrette can be refrigerated for up to 1 week. Bring to room temperature, and shake well before serving.

Ultimate Balsamic Dressing

Prep time: 5 minutes

GLUTEN-FREE, NUT-FREE, VEGETARIAN

Forget your notions about boring balsamic—this dressing is thick, rich, and entirely enticing. The secret ingredient is a tablespoon of low-sodium tamari (or soy sauce), which lends a delicious depth of flavor. I put this on everything, and I have even been known to dunk leaves of romaine directly into the jar when nobody is watching. MAKES ⅔ CUP

1 small garlic clove, peeled

3 tablespoons balsamic vinegar

1 tablespoon honey

1 tablespoon Dijon mustard

1 tablespoon low-sodium, gluten-free tamari
or soy sauce

1 teaspoon dried oregano

Kosher salt

Freshly ground black pepper

6 tablespoons extra-virgin olive oil

INGREDIENT INFO Tamari is made with fermented soybeans, like soy sauce, but is thicker, less salty, and typically contains little to no wheat. If gluten is a problem for you, always check the label to make sure your tamari contains no wheat.

1. Fit the mini food processor with the *s blade*. Add the garlic, vinegar, honey, Dijon mustard, tamari, and oregano, and season with salt and pepper. Process until smooth.

2. With the motor running, slowly drizzle the olive oil through the feed tube or through one of the holes in the lid. Taste and season with additional salt and pepper as needed.

STORAGE The vinaigrette can be refrigerated for up to 1 week. Bring to room temperature and shake well before serving.

House Dressing

Prep time: 10 minutes

GLUTEN-FREE, NUT-FREE, VEGETARIAN

When I was a kid, one of my mom's favorite special-occasion restaurants was a place called The Greenery. She adored their house dressing and begged the recipe from the chef, which she's tinkered with throughout the years. She would make the dressing for special occasions and dinner parties when I was growing up, but it's also great for every day. The secret is in the mix of dried spices, which are all things you probably already have hiding in your spice cabinet. MAKES ABOUT ¾ CUP

1 garlic clove, peeled

¼ cup red wine vinegar

2 tablespoons sugar

2 tablespoons sour cream

1 teaspoon mayonnaise

1 tablespoon milk

¼ teaspoon chili powder

¼ teaspoon paprika

¼ teaspoon dried yellow mustard

¼ teaspoon dried tarragon

¼ teaspoon salt

¼ teaspoon freshly ground black pepper

½ cup extra-virgin olive oil

1. Fit the mini food processor with the *s blade*. Add the garlic, vinegar, sugar, sour cream, mayonnaise, milk, chili powder, paprika, mustard, tarragon, salt, and pepper. Process until smooth.

2. With the motor running, slowly drizzle the olive oil through the feed tube or through one of the holes in the lid. Taste and season with additional salt and pepper as needed.

STORAGE The dressing can be refrigerated for up to 5 days. Bring to room temperature and shake well before serving.

Caesar Dressing

Prep time: 10 minutes

GLUTEN-FREE, NUT-FREE

Caesar dressing is how I learned to love salad as a kid. Creamy and rich with an unbeatable salty and savory edge, it's the perfect bedmate with crispy romaine lettuce, nutty Parmesan cheese, and crunchy croutons. You won't believe how easy it is to whip up at home—and I promise you that the flavor is a world away from the processed bottled stuff. Although the dressing is made with anchovies and raw egg yolks, have no fear. While alone they might seem forbidding, together they're as approachable as a happily married couple. MAKES ABOUT 1 CUP

1 garlic clove, peeled

2 large egg yolks

5 oil-packed anchovy fillets, drained and rinsed

2 tablespoons freshly squeezed lemon juice

1 teaspoon Dijon mustard

¼ cup grapeseed or canola oil

¼ cup extra-virgin olive oil

3 tablespoons freshly grated Parmesan cheese

Kosher salt

Freshly ground black pepper

STORAGE The dressing can be stored in the refrigerator for up to 1 day.

1. Fit the mini food processor with the *s blade*. Add the garlic, and process to chop.

2. Add the egg yolks, anchovies, lemon juice, and mustard. Process until smooth, stopping and scraping down the sides occasionally.

3. Combine the grapeseed and olive oils in a liquid measuring cup. With the motor running, very slowly drizzle in the oils through the feed tube or through one of the holes in the lid. Process until the oil is gone and the dressing is emulsified and thick.

4. Stop and scrape down the sides, and add the grated Parmesan cheese. Season with salt and pepper. Pulse to combine. Taste and season with additional salt and pepper as needed.

Buttermilk-Herb Dressing

Prep time: 10 minutes

GLUTEN-FREE, NUT-FREE, VEGETARIAN

The first time I tested this dressing, my five-year-old cleaned her salad plate, then refused to eat her dinner unless she had more salad. If you knew my daughter's, let's say, lack of enthusiasm for vegetables, you would understand how monumental this was. In fact, we all found ourselves licking our salad plates clean, then pouring the leftover dressing over our salmon and rice. It's light and vibrant—a perfect pairing with everything from garden greens, to sweet peas and asparagus, to salmon and chicken. MAKES 1 CUP

1 small garlic clove, peeled
1 tablespoon lightly packed fresh basil leaves
1 tablespoon coarsely chopped scallions
2 teaspoons freshly squeezed lemon juice
½ cup buttermilk
¼ cup Greek yogurt (preferably 2% fat)
3 tablespoons mayonnaise
    (preferably full fat)
½ teaspoon sugar
1 teaspoon extra-virgin olive oil
Kosher salt
Freshly ground black pepper

1. Fit the mini food processor with the *s blade*. Add the garlic, basil, scallions, and lemon juice. Process until coarsely chopped. Stop and scrape down the sides.

2. Add the buttermilk, Greek yogurt, mayonnaise, sugar, olive oil, and a big pinch of salt and pepper. Process until smooth. Taste and season with additional salt and pepper as needed.

STORAGE The dressing can be refrigerated for up to 3 days.

Smoky-Sweet Spice Rub

Prep time: 5 minutes

GLUTEN-FREE, NUT-FREE, VEGAN

With a touch of smokiness from paprika, sweetness from brown sugar, and lots of garlic, this spice rub enhances nearly any meat. I like to slather it on steaks or cuts of pork before grilling, but it's also great on a sliced block of tofu if eating meat isn't your thing. If you have the time, refrigerate the meat or tofu with the rub for several hours, or even overnight, before grilling. The rub is also awesome with grilled or roasted shrimp. MAKES ABOUT ⅓ CUP

3 garlic cloves, peeled

2 tablespoons smoked paprika

1 tablespoon packed light brown sugar

1 tablespoon lemon zest
(about 2 lemons)

1½ teaspoons kosher salt

¼ teaspoon black pepper

1. Fit the mini food processor with the *s blade*. Add the garlic, and process to finely chop. Stop and scrape down the sides.

2. Add the smoked paprika, brown sugar, lemon zest, salt, and pepper. Process until well combined.

STORAGE The spice rub can be refrigerated for up to 3 days.

Fajita Rub

Prep time: 5 minutes

GLUTEN-FREE, NUT-FREE, VEGAN

I originally developed this recipe to slather on a pork shoulder before slow cooking it to tender perfection, then shredding it and piling it into taco shells. However, I discovered that it's also awesome on roasted salmon, chicken, or veggies which we layer into fajitas. The rub will give your fajitas a kick of heat, as well as some sweetness from the addition of brown sugar and cinnamon. MAKES ABOUT ⅓ CUP

3 garlic cloves, peeled
2 tablespoons chili powder
2 teaspoons ground cumin
2 teaspoons ground coriander
1 teaspoon dried oregano
1 teaspoon ground cinnamon
2 teaspoons brown sugar
1 tablespoon kosher salt

1. Fit the mini food processor with the *s blade*. Add the garlic, and process to chop. Stop and scrape down the sides.

2. Add the chili powder, cumin, coriander, oregano, cinnamon, brown sugar, and salt, and process until well combined.

STORAGE The spice rub can be refrigerated for up to 3 days.

Garlic-Herb Butter

Prep time: 5 minutes

GLUTEN-FREE, NUT-FREE, VEGETARIAN

Having this garlic-herb butter in your fridge is like owning a magic wand. It instantly transforms simple, ordinary dishes into something special, and it's great for last-minute meals. You can slather it on steamed ears of corn, rub it under the skin of a chicken before roasting, serve it on top of grilled fish or grilled meats, toss it with pasta and Parmesan cheese, or even spread it on French bread before baking for the ultimate garlic bread. Whatever it touches, it makes better. MAKES ½ CUP

2 garlic cloves, peeled

2 tablespoons coarsely chopped scallions

2 tablespoons coarsely chopped fresh parsley

1 stick butter, at room temperature

Kosher salt

Freshly ground black pepper

1. Fit the mini food processor with the *s blade*. Add the garlic, and process until finely chopped. Add the scallions and parsley. Process until finely chopped. Stop and scrape down the sides.

2. Add the butter, and season with salt and pepper. Process to incorporate the butter, stopping and scraping down the sides as needed.

3. You can either use the butter immediately or transfer it to a large piece of plastic wrap, wrap it into a log, and refrigerate.

STORAGE The butter can be refrigerated for up to 1 week.

Condiments, Spreads, Dips & Doughs

Guacamole

Prep time: 5 minutes

GLUTEN-FREE, NUT-FREE, VEGAN

We all know how to smash avocados—all you need is a big fork. But if you're making a large batch of guacamole, this is the way to do it. Everything gets dumped into the processor and blitzed in seconds. It literally cut my prep time in half. Rinsing the chopped onion removes some of its bite, so don't skip this step. This recipe is especially brilliant for parties. Let the fiesta begin! MAKES ABOUT 2 CUPS

1 garlic clove, peeled

1 jalapeño pepper (red or green), seeded, inner ribs discarded

¼ red onion, coarsely chopped and rinsed

¼ cup lightly packed fresh cilantro leaves

3 ripe avocados, halved and pitted

2 to 3 tablespoons freshly squeezed lime juice

Salt

Freshly ground black pepper

INGREDIENT INFO I was always taught to add an avocado pit to the guacamole to prevent it from turning brown. Myth debunked! Apparently, this is an old wives' tale. The best way to prevent oxidation is to place plastic wrap directly on the surface, to keep any air from touching it.

1. Fit the food processor with the s *blade.* With the motor running, drop the garlic clove through the feed tube, followed by the jalapeño. Process until finely chopped. Stop and scrape down the sides.

2. Add the onion and cilantro, and pulse until finely chopped, about 10 to 15 pulses. Stop and scrape down the sides.

3. Scoop out the flesh from the avocados, and add it to the food processor, along with 2 tablespoons of lime juice. Season with salt and pepper. Pulse until the avocado is smashed according to your liking (some like it chunky; some like it smooth). Taste, season with additional salt, pepper, or lime juice as needed, and serve.

STORAGE The guacamole can be left at room temperature for up to an hour or refrigerated for up to a day. Place a piece of plastic wrap directly on the surface to prevent it from turning brown. If it does turn brown, simply scrape off and discard the surface.

Homemade Ketchup

Prep time: 15 minutes • Cook time: about 75 minutes

GLUTEN-FREE, NUT-FREE, VEGAN

I admit I was wary about making my own ketchup. After all, who can beat the bottled stuff? But after I gave it a try, I couldn't believe the freshness of flavor. It's so good: sweet, slightly vinegary, and a tad spicy. It takes our burgers—and fries, and chicken cutlets, and eggs— to whole new heights, without the addition of the high-fructose corn syrup typically found in bottled brands. While it takes a bit of time to simmer on the stove, most of the work is hands-off. MAKES ABOUT 1¼ CUPS

4 cups seeded and chopped plum tomatoes
(about 6 large tomatoes)

1 cup raw apple cider vinegar

½ cup packed dark brown sugar

1 tablespoon kosher salt

⅛ teaspoon ground cinnamon

⅛ teaspoon ground allspice

1 teaspoon freshly ground black pepper

¼ teaspoon Worcestershire sauce
(make sure it's gluten-free if needed)

INGREDIENT INFO Do you like it spicy? For ketchup with a kick, add another teaspoon of freshly ground black pepper.

1. In a medium saucepan over high heat, bring the tomatoes, vinegar, sugar, salt, cinnamon, allspice, and pepper to a boil, then reduce to a simmer and cook until thick and slightly syrupy, about 75 minutes.

2. Fit the food processor with the *s blade*. Transfer the mixture to the processor, and add the Worcestershire sauce. Process until completely smooth, stopping and scraping down the sides occasionally. Refrigerate until chilled.

STORAGE The ketchup can be stored in the refrigerator for up to 1 month.

Classic Mayonnaise

Prep time: 10 minutes

GLUTEN-FREE, NUT-FREE, VEGETARIAN

My husband's uncle, John Daniel Reaves, is a born and raised Southern gentleman, as well as a great cook with a serious love for his food processor. He's been using it since the 1970s for Southern classics such as biscuits, Roasted Red Pepper Cheese Spread (page 68), and home-made mayonnaise. His mayonnaise recipe is smooth, velvety, and bright. It takes any ordinary sandwich to totally new heights. Warning: Once you try this, you won't want to go back to the jarred stuff! MAKES ABOUT 1 ¼ CUPS

1 large egg

1 teaspoon dry Colman's mustard

1 tablespoon Champagne vinegar

Juice of ½ lemon

1 teaspoon kosher salt

Pinch ground cayenne pepper

1 cup grapeseed or canola oil

STORAGE The mayonnaise can be refrigerated for up to 1 week.

1. Fit the mini food processor with the *s blade*. Add the egg, mustard, vinegar, lemon juice, salt, and cayenne. Pulse to combine.

2. With the motor running, very slowly start adding the grapeseed oil, drop by drop, through the feed tube or through one of the holes in the lid. Continue adding the oil in a slow, steady stream. When about half the oil has been added, stop the machine to let the motor rest for a few seconds. Start the motor, and continue adding the oil slowly until it is completely incorporated and the mixture is thick and velvety. Taste and season with additional salt as needed.

Garlic Aioli

Prep time: 10 minutes

GLUTEN-FREE, NUT-FREE, VEGETARIAN

This is basically a mayonnaise, flavored with garlic and extra-virgin olive oil. It's incredible with fish, seafood, and vegetables. A microplane is a grater with very fine teeth. By grating the garlic instead of chopping it in the food processor, you'll end up with a smoother aioli. MAKES ABOUT 1¼ CUPS

2 garlic cloves, peeled

1 large egg

1 teaspoon Dijon mustard

1 tablespoon Champagne vinegar

Juice of ½ lemon

1 teaspoon kosher salt

Pinch ground cayenne pepper

½ cup grapeseed or canola oil

½ cup extra-virgin olive oil

STORAGE The garlic aioli can be refrigerated for up to 1 week.

SIMPLE SWAP For a flavored variation, try stirring in a teaspoon of finely chopped fresh herbs, such as basil, thyme, parsley, or chives.

1. Using a microplane, grate the garlic cloves; set aside.

2. Fit the mini food processor with the *s blade*. Add the egg, mustard, vinegar, lemon juice, salt, and cayenne. Pulse to combine.

3. With the motor running, very slowly start adding the grapeseed oil, drop by drop, through the feed tube or through one of the holes in the lid. Continue adding the oil in a slow, steady stream. When all of the grapeseed oil has been added, stop the machine to let the motor rest for a few seconds. Start the motor, and slowly add the olive oil, processing until all of the oil has been incorporated and the mixture is thick and velvety.

4. Scrape in the grated garlic, and pulse to combine. Taste and season with additional salt as needed.

Tapenade

Prep time: 10 minutes

GLUTEN-FREE, NUT-FREE

This Provençal paste of olives, garlic, capers, and anchovies is intensely flavorful. It makes a delicious appetizer spread over French bread or—my personal favorite—spooned over goat cheese on a crostini. It's also great stuffed inside chicken breasts before roasting. No canned olives, please; go for good-quality whole olives—the kind you find in the olive bar or specialty deli section of the grocery store. Niçoise, Kalamata, and picholine olives are all good choices. MAKES ABOUT ¾ CUP

2 anchovy fillets, rinsed

1 garlic clove, peeled

1 tablespoon coarsely chopped fresh basil

1 tablespoon coarsely chopped fresh parsley

1 cup mixed whole olives (8 ounces),
   rinsed and pitted

1 tablespoon capers

1 tablespoon freshly squeezed lemon juice

3 tablespoons extra-virgin olive oil

Freshly ground black pepper

1. Fit the mini food processor with the *s blade*. Add the anchovies and garlic. Process to finely chop.

2. Add the basil, parsley, olives, capers, lemon juice, and olive oil, and season with pepper. Pulse to a coarse paste, about 12 to 15 pulses. Transfer to a bowl, and serve.

STORAGE The tapenade can be refrigerated for up to 1 week.

HOW-TO To pit olives, you don't need any special equipment, just a big knife. Place 2 or 3 olives on a cutting board, and, using the flat part of the knife, press down on (or smack) the olives until they crack open. Then simply pull out the pits.

"Go Bears!" Dip
(Sriracha Cream Cheese Dip)

Prep time: 5 minutes

GLUTEN-FREE, NUT-FREE, VEGETARIAN

My good friends Kelley and Amanda are avid Chicago Bears football fans. They started making this simple but insanely addictive dip to nosh on while watching the games. Their son started calling it "Go Bears!" dip when he was a toddler, and the name has stuck. While I must admit that I'm not a football fan, this dip is enough to get me to watch a game—at least until the bowl empties. The recipe can be halved, by the way, if you're not serving a crowd. MAKES ABOUT 2¼ CUPS

2 large garlic cloves, peeled

2 (8-ounce) packages cream cheese, at room temperature

½ cup sour cream

2 to 3 tablespoons sriracha sauce, plus more for drizzling

Kosher salt

Potato chips (preferably a sturdy ridged or kettle chip), for serving (make sure they're gluten-free if needed)

INGREDIENT INFO Sriracha is a hot chili sauce that originated in Thailand. It's made primarily with chiles, garlic, vinegar, salt, and sugar. It's slightly sweet, spicy, and acidic. We drizzle it on almost everything, from eggs to curries, noodles, rice, and burgers.

1. Fit the food processor with the s blade. With the motor running, drop the garlic through the feed tube to chop.

2. Add the cream cheese, sour cream, and 2 tablespoons of sriracha, and season with salt. Process until smooth, stopping and scraping down the sides occasionally. Taste and pulse in an additional tablespoon of sriracha, if you prefer it spicier. Transfer to a bowl, and drizzle with more sriracha. Serve with potato chips for dipping.

STORAGE The dip can be refrigerated for up to 5 days. Bring to room temperature before serving.

Pea and Goat Cheese Spread

Prep time: 10 minutes

GLUTEN-FREE, NUT-FREE, VEGETARIAN

I developed this recipe on a freezing cold day in March when I was desperately craving spring. Since fresh garden peas were still months away, I used defrosted frozen peas, which I buzzed in the processor with garlic, goat cheese, Parmesan, herbs, and lemon juice. The result was a creamy, vibrant spread that tasted of spring, even though there was still snow on the ground. The spread is fantastic on French bread or crostini, and it's a delicious dip for veggies (think fennel spears, endives, radishes, and baby carrots). It's even great tossed with pasta. MAKES 1¼ CUPS

1 garlic clove, peeled

1½ cups defrosted frozen peas

2 ounces goat cheese

1 tablespoon chopped fresh herbs, such as mint, basil, tarragon, and/or thyme

1 tablespoon grated Parmesan cheese

1 tablespoon freshly squeezed lemon juice

1 tablespoon water

Salt

Freshly ground black pepper

1 tablespoon extra-virgin olive oil

1. Fit the food processor with the *s blade*. With the motor running, drop the garlic through the feed tube to chop.

2. Add the peas along with the goat cheese, herbs, Parmesan cheese, lemon juice, water, and a pinch of salt and pepper. Process to a slightly chunky purée, stopping and scraping down the sides occasionally.

3. Add the olive oil, and process until just combined. Taste, season with additional salt and pepper as needed, and serve.

STORAGE The spread can be stored in the refrigerator for up to 2 days.

Green Goodness Avocado Dip

Prep time: 10 minutes

GLUTEN-FREE, NUT-FREE, VEGAN

Dip a few carrots into it. Slather it on a cracker. Drizzle it over salad greens. This thick, green "goodness" is as versatile as it is delicious. It's also incredibly healthy. Made with a base of garlic and herbs, then thickened with avocado and spiked with a hint of lemon juice and raw apple cider vinegar, it's creamy and luscious, but filled with the good stuff. MAKES ABOUT ¾ CUP

1 garlic clove, peeled
1 scallion, coarsely chopped
⅓ cup packed fresh basil leaves
⅓ cup packed fresh parsley leaves
2 tablespoons freshly squeezed lemon juice
1 tablespoon raw apple cider vinegar
2 tablespoons water
Kosher salt
Freshly ground black pepper
1 medium avocado, halved and pitted
2 tablespoons extra-virgin olive oil

1. Fit the mini food processor with the *s blade*. Add the garlic, and process to chop. Stop and scrape down the sides.

2. Add the scallion, basil, parsley, lemon juice, vinegar, and water. Season with salt and pepper. Process until the herbs are finely chopped.

3. Scoop the avocado flesh into the processor, and process until smooth. Slowly add the olive oil with the machine running. Taste, season with additional salt and pepper as needed, and serve.

STORAGE The dip can refrigerated for up to 2 days.

Hummus

Prep time: 10 minutes

GLUTEN-FREE, NUT-FREE, VEGAN

We eat a lot of hummus in my house. It's our go-to snack every evening, when we're all starving before dinner and blood sugar is running low (meaning that whining is running high). I'll set out a bowl of hummus and some raw vegetables and watch as my five-year-old actually eats something other than carbohydrates. Once you start making your own hummus at home, it's hard to go back to the packaged stuff. Not only is it much cheaper, but the flavor is incomparable. MAKES ABOUT 1½ CUPS

1 garlic clove, peeled

1 (15-ounce) can chickpeas, reserve
   2 tablespoons of liquid from the can,
   drain, and rinse

2 tablespoons tahini

2 tablespoons freshly squeezed lemon juice

Kosher salt

2 tablespoons extra-virgin olive oil,
   plus more for serving

Ground sumac or chili powder,
   for sprinkling (optional)

STORAGE The hummus can be refrigerated for up to 1 week.

1. Fit the food processor with the *s blade*. With the motor running, drop the garlic clove through the feed tube to chop. Stop and scrape down the sides.

2. Add the chickpeas, tahini, lemon juice, and the reserved chickpea liquid, and season with salt. Process until smooth, stopping and scraping down the sides occasionally.

3. With the motor running, slowly drizzle the olive oil through the feed tube. Process until combined. If you prefer a thinner hummus, add another tablespoon or two of water. Taste and season with additional salt as needed.

4. Before serving, drizzle the hummus with more olive oil and sprinkle with ground sumac or chili powder, if you wish.

Babaganoush

Prep time: 15 minutes • Cook time: 45 minutes

GLUTEN-FREE, NUT-FREE, VEGAN

Babaganoush is not only fun to say, it's also fun to make and surprisingly simple. Whole eggplants go straight into a hot oven (or onto a grill) and, after cooking, the remaining prep is just like making hummus. The eggplant flesh gets processed with tahini, lemon juice, garlic, and olive oil, until you end up with a creamy dip that's irresistible with warm pita bread or slices of crisp cucumber. MAKES ABOUT 2¾ CUPS

2 or 3 medium Italian eggplants
  (about 2 pounds)

2 garlic cloves, peeled

3 tablespoons freshly squeezed lemon juice

3 tablespoons tahini

Kosher salt

Freshly ground black pepper

1 tablespoon extra-virgin olive oil,
  plus more for serving

2 tablespoons chopped fresh parsley

STORAGE The babaganoush can be refrigerated for up to 1 week.

1. Preheat the oven to 450°F.

2. Place the eggplants on a foil-lined baking sheet, and bake in the top third of the oven for 15 minutes. Turn them over and bake 15 to 25 minutes more, or until charred on the outside and soft in the center. Cover tightly with foil, and let sit 15 minutes to steam.

3. Fit the food processor with the *s blade*. With the motor running, drop the garlic cloves through the feed tube to chop.

4. Halve the eggplants vertically. Scoop out the flesh and seeds, and transfer to the food processor (discard the skins). Add the lemon juice and tahini, and season with salt and pepper. Process to a coarse paste, stopping and scraping down the sides occasionally.

5. With the motor running, slowly drizzle in the olive oil. Add the parsley, and pulse to combine. Taste and season with additional salt as needed.

6. Transfer to a bowl, and drizzle with a bit more olive oil before serving.

COOKING TIP To grill the eggplants, preheat a grill to medium. Place the eggplants on the grill and rotate occasionally until they're charred on the outside and softened in the middle, about 30 to 40 minutes. Cover tightly with foil, and let sit 15 minutes to steam, then proceed with step 3.

Creamy Herbed Vegetable Dip

Prep time: 5 minutes

GLUTEN-FREE, NUT-FREE, VEGETARIAN

If I had a signature dip, this would be it. It's creamy and cooling, with tons of flavor from fresh herbs, garlic, and crumbled goat cheese or feta. You can use whatever herbs you have or like. I find it's best to use Greek yogurt with at least 2% fat. If you use nonfat yogurt, you might want to add a teaspoon or two of olive oil to round out the tartness. While this was developed as a vegetable dip, it's also awesome with potato chips. MAKES 1 ¼ CUPS

1 garlic clove, peeled

½ cup plain Greek yogurt (preferably 2% fat)

½ cup crème fraîche

½ teaspoon freshly squeezed lemon juice

Kosher salt

Freshly ground black pepper

2 tablespoons thinly sliced scallions

1 tablespoon finely chopped fresh herbs, such as parsley, mint, dill, basil, and/or oregano

⅓ cup crumbled goat cheese or feta

Sliced vegetables, such as carrots, radishes, fennel, cucumber, blanched broccoli, and red peppers, for dipping

STORAGE The dip can be refrigerated for up to 3 days.

1. Fit the mini food processor with the *s blade*. Add the garlic, and process to finely chop. Add the yogurt, crème fraîche, and lemon juice, and season with salt and pepper. Process until smooth, stopping and scraping down the sides occasionally.

2. Add the scallions, herbs, and goat cheese. Pulse to combine. Taste and season with additional salt and pepper as needed.

3. Transfer the dip to a bowl, and serve with sliced vegetables for dipping.

SIMPLE SWAP If you don't have Greek yogurt, you can use regular plain yogurt. Drain it first, so it will be thick like the Greek variety. Line a fine mesh sieve with cheesecloth or a coffee filter, and set it over a bowl. Place the plain yogurt in the sieve, and stick the whole thing in the refrigerator to let the liquid drain, about 2 to 4 hours.

Tuscan White Bean Dip

Prep time: 10 minutes

GLUTEN-FREE, NUT-FREE, VEGAN

When we have friends over for dinner, I like to do as much as I can ahead of time. Fussy, last minute hors d'oeuvres disappeared with the arrival of my kids. Instead, I set out a few simple but delicious nibbles that we can snack on with drinks. This white bean dip is wonderful with sliced vegetables (whatever is in season), crackers, or bread. If I'm feeling a bit fancy, I'll spread it on crostini, top it with sautéed spinach, and garnish with a shaving or two of Parmesan. I've also been known to eat that for lunch. MAKES ABOUT 1 ¼ CUPS

1 garlic clove, peeled

1 (15-ounce) can cannellini beans, drained and rinsed

1 teaspoon minced fresh rosemary

1 teaspoon minced fresh thyme

1 tablespoon minced fresh parsley

⅛ teaspoon red pepper flakes

½ teaspoon lemon zest

Juice of 1 lemon, divided

¼ cup water

Kosher salt

Freshly ground black pepper

3 tablespoons good-quality extra-virgin olive oil, plus more for serving

Sliced vegetables, such as carrots, cucumber slices, fennel spears, radishes, and blanched green beans, or crostini, for dipping

STORAGE The dip can be refrigerated for up to 5 days. Bring to room temperature before serving.

1. Fit the food processor with the *s blade*. With the motor running, drop the garlic clove through the feed tube to chop. Stop and scrape down the sides.

2. Add the cannellini beans, rosemary, thyme, parsley, red pepper flakes, lemon zest, the juice of ½ lemon, and water. Season with salt and pepper, and purée until smooth. Stop and scrape down the sides.

3. Add the olive oil, and purée until just combined. Taste and add additional lemon juice, salt or pepper as needed.

4. Transfer the dip to a serving bowl, drizzle with a bit more olive oil, and serve with assorted vegetables and crackers or over crostini.

Roasted Red Pepper Cheese Spread

Prep time: 30 minutes • Cook time: 10 minutes

GLUTEN-FREE OPTION, NUT-FREE, VEGETARIAN

Full disclosure—this is really just pimento cheese spread. The recipe comes from my husband's uncle, John Daniel Reaves, the mayonnaise master, (Classic Mayonnaise page 56), who adapted the recipe from Southern cooking master Frank Stitt. Sharp Cheddar cheese gets mixed with roasted red peppers, cream cheese, and seasonings (the garlic is my touch) for a startlingly addicting spread for crackers or bread. It also makes fantastic lunch box sandwiches. MAKES ABOUT 4 CUPS

Extra-virgin olive oil or cooking spray, for greasing

3 red bell peppers

1 pound sharp Cheddar cheese

1 small garlic clove, peeled

4 ounces cream cheese

⅓ cup Classic Mayonnaise (page 56)

1 teaspoon freshly squeezed lemon juice

Pinch ground cayenne pepper

1 teaspoon sugar

Kosher salt

Freshly ground black pepper

Crackers or bread, for serving (make sure they're gluten-free if needed)

1. Preheat the broiler to high, and place a rack 5 to 6 inches from the heating element. Line a baking sheet with foil, and brush it lightly with the olive oil.

2. Halve the peppers, and remove and discard the seeds and ribs. Arrange the peppers, cut-side down, on the baking sheet. Broil until blackened, about 10 minutes. Cover with foil, and let sit 10 minutes to steam. Remove and discard the skins and stems from the peppers. Coarsely chop.

3. Fit the food processor with the *shredding disc*. Push the Cheddar cheese through the feed tube to shred. Transfer to a bowl.

4. Reassemble the food processor with the s *blade* (no need to wash). With the motor running, drop the garlic clove through the feed tube to chop. Stop and scrape down the sides.

5. Add the cream cheese, mayonnaise, lemon juice, cayenne, and sugar, and season with salt and pepper. Process until smooth, stopping and scraping down the sides occasionally. Add the roasted red peppers, and process until well incorporated. Stop and scrape down the sides.

6. Add the grated cheese, and pulse until incorporated, about 15 pulses. Taste and season with additional salt and pepper as needed. Transfer to a serving dish, and refrigerate until chilled. Serve with crackers or bread.

STORAGE The spread can be refrigerated for up to 1 week.

Tomatillo Salsa, Two Ways

Prep time: 15 minutes • Cook time: 10 minutes

GLUTEN-FREE, NUT-FREE, VEGAN

Fresh tomatillos have a tart, chipper flavor with notes of lime. They're a staple in Mexican cuisine, and they're the basis of Mexican salsa verde, or green salsa. Here you'll find two versions—one using raw tomatillos and one using broiled. The raw version is a bit more herbal and citrusy, while the roasted version is richer and a tad more complex. Use the salsas as a dip for chips, serve them over tacos, or try them in the Chicken, Greens, and Goat Cheese Quesadillas (page 176). MAKES 1 CUP EACH

1 garlic clove, peeled

5 or 6 medium tomatillos (about 8 ounces), husked and rinsed

1 jalapeño pepper

¼ medium onion

¼ cup lightly packed fresh cilantro leaves

1 tablespoon freshly squeezed lime juice

Kosher salt

TO MAKE FRESH TOMATILLO SALSA

1. Fit the food processor with the *s blade*. Coarsely chop the garlic, tomatillos, and jalapeño (you can either remove the jalapeño seeds and ribs for a milder salsa or keep them in for a spicier version), and add them to the food processor.

2. Coarsely chop the onion, and give it a rinse in cold water. Add the onion to the processor, along with the cilantro and lime juice. Season with salt.

3. Process to a coarse purée, stopping and scraping down the sides occasionally. Taste and season with additional salt as needed.

4. Drain the salsa briefly in a strainer to remove excess liquid before serving.

TO MAKE ROASTED TOMATILLO SALSA

1. Preheat a broiler to high. Line a baking sheet with aluminum foil.

2. Arrange the garlic clove, tomatillos, jalapeño, and onion in a single layer on the baking sheet, and broil until roasted and lightly blackened in spots, about 5 minutes. Turn the vegetables over, and broil for another 4 to 5 minutes, or until blistered and lightly blackened.

3. Cut off and discard the stem of the jalapeño (you can either remove the jalapeño seeds and ribs for a milder salsa or keep them in for a spicier version).

4. Fit the food processor with the *s blade*. Transfer the jalapeño, along with the broiled vegetables and any juices, to the food processor. Add the cilantro and lime juice, and season with salt. Process to a coarse purée, stopping and scraping down the sides occasionally. Serve.

STORAGE The tomatillo salsas can be stored in an airtight container in the refrigerator for up to 1 week.

INGREDIENT INFO Tomatillos are a member of the nightshade family (they're cousins to tomatoes, eggplants, and potatoes). They're sold in their husks, which need to be removed. The skins tend to be sticky, so give them a wash before using.

Fresh Tomato Salsa

Prep time: 10 minutes, plus 10 minutes to sit

GLUTEN-FREE, NUT-FREE, VEGAN

My dad isn't much of a cook (sorry, Dad!), but he was in charge of the grill when I was growing up. One night when he was on dinner duty, he made a fresh tomato salsa to accompany grilled sea bass. The combination of the warm, smoky fish with the cool salsa became his signature dish. I've adapted his tomato salsa using the food processor, which cuts the prep time in half. Serve it over grilled fish, in tacos, or with tortilla chips for dipping. The salsa will taste best with ripe summer tomatoes. MAKES ABOUT 2½ CUPS

1 garlic clove, peeled

1 jalapeño pepper, halved, seeded, and inner ribs discarded

¼ red onion, coarsely chopped and rinsed in cold water

¼ cup lightly packed fresh cilantro leaves

5 plum tomatoes, cored, seeded, and coarsely chopped

Kosher salt

Freshly ground black pepper

Juice of ½ lime

1 teaspoon extra-virgin olive oil

TIME SAVER This salsa calls for tomatoes that have had their seeds removed. To do this, halve the tomatoes lengthwise. Working over a bowl, give the tomatoes a gentle squeeze to get rid of some of their liquid. Then use your fingers or a spoon to scoop out the remaining seeds.

1. Fit the food processor with the *s blade*. With the motor running, drop the garlic clove through the feed tube, followed by the jalapeño halves. Process until finely chopped. Stop and scrape down the sides.

2. Add the onion and cilantro. Pulse until finely chopped, about 10 to 15 pulses. Add the tomatoes, and season with salt and pepper. Pulse just until the tomatoes are coarsely chopped, 5 to 8 pulses. Transfer to a strainer to drain off excess liquid.

3. Transfer the salsa to a bowl, and stir in the lime juice and olive oil. Taste and season with additional salt and pepper as needed. Let sit at least 10 minutes so the flavors meld before serving.

STORAGE The salsa can be refrigerated for up to 3 days.

Homemade
Peanut Butter

Prep time: 10 minutes

GLUTEN-FREE, VEGAN

Dump peanuts in a food processor with salt. Turn it on. Ta da! *In five minutes, you have the creamiest, smoothest peanut butter you could imagine, at a fraction of the cost of jarred nut or seed butters. Best of all, you can control the amount of sweetener, if you wish to add any at all. Feel free to get creative with the flavorings. I love maple-cinnamon peanut butter with a pinch of cayenne pepper for some unexpected heat.* MAKES ABOUT 1 ¼ CUPS

2½ cups roasted, unsalted peanuts

½ teaspoon kosher salt

Optional add-ins:

1 tablespoon maple syrup or sugar
   (or honey if not vegan)

⅛ to ¼ teaspoon ground cinnamon or
   other spices

SIMPLE SWAP If you can't find roasted, unsalted peanuts, you can buy raw peanuts and roast them in a 300°F oven for 10 to 20 minutes, or until golden and fragrant.

1. Fit the food processor with the *s blade*. Add the peanuts and salt, and process for 5 to 6 minutes, stopping and scraping down the sides occasionally, until the mixture is completely smooth, creamy, and runny (it will first seize up into a ball, but don't worry; it will smooth out).

2. If you'd like, add a tablespoon of sweetener or season with a touch of spice. Process again until smooth. Transfer the peanut butter to a clean jar or container and refrigerate.

STORAGE The peanut butter can be refrigerated for up to 2 months.

Roasted Almond or Cashew Butter

Prep time: 10 to 15 minutes • Cook time: 10 to 15 minutes

GLUTEN-FREE, VEGAN

Once you start making your own nut butter, you won't want to go back to buying it in jars. Freshly roasted nuts are processed into a silky smooth butter without the addition of any extra oils. They have a fresh, pure flavor—and let's not forget how much cheaper it is to make them at home. After the nuts are roasted, the food processor does all the work. Be sure to use a standard-size processor, as the motor on the mini processors isn't strong enough. Feel free to experiment with different sweeteners and spices. MAKES 1½ CUPS

3 cups raw cashews or almonds

½ teaspoon kosher salt

Optional add-ins:

1 tablespoon maple syrup or sugar
   (or honey if not vegan)

⅛ to ¼ teaspoon ground cinnamon or
   other spices

STORAGE The roasted nut butters can be refrigerated for up to 2 months.

1. Preheat the oven to 350°F. Spread the nuts on a baking sheet in a single layer, and bake until lightly toasted and fragrant, stirring once or twice, about 12 to 14 minutes for almonds and 8 to 10 minutes for cashews.

2. Fit the food processor with the *s blade*. Carefully add the warm nuts (warm nuts will make the process go faster). Add the salt, and process for 10 to 15 minutes, stopping and scraping down the sides occasionally, or until the mixture is smooth, creamy, and runny (it will first seize up into a ball, but don't worry; it will smooth out).

3. If you'd like, add a tablespoon of sweetener or season with a touch of spice. Process again until smooth. Transfer the nut butter to a clean jar or container and refrigerate.

Pizza Dough

Prep time: 10 minutes, plus 1 hour, 15 minutes to rise

NUT-FREE, VEGETARIAN

Homemade pizzas from scratch on a weekday? Yes you can! This ultra simple dough comes together with the help of the food processor in just 10 minutes. You can either make the dough on the same day—it needs about an hour to rise before baking—or you can make it the day before and let it rise overnight in the refrigerator. MAKES 4 (9-INCH) PIZZAS

1 teaspoon sugar

1 tablespoon active dry yeast

1 cup warm water (105° to 115°F; it should feel lukewarm to the touch)

3 cups all-purpose flour, plus more for flouring

1 teaspoon kosher salt

1½ tablespoons extra-virgin olive oil

INGREDIENT INFO Active dry vs. rapid rise— are these yeasts interchangeable? The answer, unfortunately, is no. Rapid-rise yeast has been processed into smaller particles that don't need to be dissolved in water, but it won't give you the same structure and flavor the active dry yeast in this recipe.

1. In a medium bowl or measuring cup, dissolve the sugar and yeast in the warm water (I do this in a liquid measuring cup with a spout, for easier pouring later). Let stand until foamy, about 5 minutes.

2. Fit the food processor with the *s blade*. Add the flour and salt. Pulse to combine. With the motor running, pour the yeast mixture through the feed tube, followed by the olive oil. Continue processing until the dough forms a ball along the side of the bowl, about 1 minute. Process for 1 minute longer.

3. Scrape the dough out onto a lightly floured surface, and knead it 2 or 3 times to form a smooth ball. Divide the dough into 4 equal pieces. Form each piece into a ball. ➡

IF YOU'RE MAKING THE PIZZAS RIGHT AWAY

Place the dough balls on a lightly floured surface and cover with a lightly damp dish towel. Let rise until almost doubled in size, about 1 hour and 15 minutes.

IF YOU'RE MAKING THE PIZZAS TOMORROW

Place the dough balls on a lightly floured, parchment-lined baking sheet. Be sure to give them some room to expand, as they'll almost double in size. Cover with plastic wrap, and refrigerate overnight. Let sit at room temperature for 15 minutes before shaping.

TO SHAPE THE DOUGH

Place a dough ball on a lightly floured surface and press it into a ½-inch-thick round. Using a rolling pin, roll the dough into a 9-inch round. Transfer to a parchment-lined rimless baking sheet, and top as desired (it's best to top sparingly to avoid a soggy crust). Slide the pizza (on the parchment) onto a pizza stone or bake directly on the baking sheet on the bottom rack of a 500°F oven, until the crust is golden.

Classic Pie Dough

Prep time: 10 minutes, plus 40 minutes to chill

GLUTEN-FREE OPTION, NUT-FREE, VEGETARIAN

The flavor and texture of homemade pie crust is absolutely unbeatable, and with the help of the food processor, you can master it! This crust is flaky and tender, with a rich, buttery flavor. The trick here is to use a high-quality, high-butterfat butter, such as European-style butter. This will not only enhance the flavor, but it will also make the dough much easier to work with. This is my go-to pie crust for both sweet and savory pies and tarts, and you'll use it in the recipes for Blueberry-Almond Galette (page 229) and Pumpkin Pie (page 236). For savory dishes such as the Individual Chicken Pot Pies (page 178), just omit the sugar. MAKES 1 DOUBLE-CRUST PIE OR 2 SINGLE-CRUST PIES

2½ cups all-purpose flour or gluten-free flour (I use Cup4Cup)

1 tablespoon sugar (optional)

½ teaspoon kosher salt

2 sticks cold unsalted butter, cut into ½-inch cubes

6 tablespoons ice water, plus more if needed

STORAGE The pie dough can be refrigerated for up to 24 hours, or frozen in a zip-top bag for up to 3 months. To defrost, refrigerate overnight.

1. Fit the food processor with the *s blade.* Add the flour, sugar (if using), and salt. Pulse to combine.

2. Sprinkle the cold butter over the flour, and pulse until the butter is cut into pea-size pieces, about 15 pulses.

3. Remove the lid, drizzle in the ice water, then pulse until the mixture looks sandy, about 10 to 15 pulses. Pinch the dough between your fingertips—if it holds together, you're ready to go. If not, drizzle in 1 to 2 more teaspoons of water and pulse again.

4. Transfer the dough to a work surface, such as a countertop or cutting board, and gently form it into a ball. Divide the dough into two pieces, and wrap each in plastic wrap. Flatten each piece into a disc, and wrap with another piece of plastic. Refrigerate the dough for at least 30 minutes, or up to 24 hours.

Graham Cracker Pie Dough

Prep time: 5 minutes • Cook time: 15 minutes

NUT-FREE, VEGETARIAN

This is the easiest pie dough imaginable, but arguably one of the tastiest. Use this in recipes that call for a prebaked crust, such as cheesecakes, key lime tarts, French silk pies, or Lemon Bars with Graham Cracker Crust and Whipped Cream (page 218). Best of all, there's no rolling of dough required, as the crust gets pressed directly into the baking dish or pie pan. I often add a touch of cinnamon for extra flavor. For a gluten-free version, you can use the same weight in gluten-free graham crackers. MAKES 1 (9-INCH) PIE CRUST

12 whole graham crackers (about 6½ ounces)

2 tablespoons sugar

½ teaspoon ground cinnamon (optional)

5 tablespoons butter, melted

TIME SAVER The bottom of a flat-bottomed dry measuring cup works perfectly for pressing the dough into an even layer on the bottom and sides of the baking dish.

STORAGE A prebaked graham cracker pie crust can be stored at room temperature for up to 1 day before adding the filling. Once cool, cover with plastic wrap.

1. Preheat the oven to 350°F.

2. Fit the food processor with the *s blade*. Break the graham crackers into the processor. Process until finely ground. Add the sugar and cinnamon (if using), and process until combined.

3. Pour the melted butter evenly over the crumbs. Pulse until the butter is completely incorporated and the mixture looks like wet sand. The crust is now ready to use.

4. Transfer the dough to a 9-inch pie dish. Press it evenly onto the bottom and up the sides of the dish.

5. Bake until lightly golden and fragrant, about 10 to 15 minutes. Cool on a wire rack before adding the filling.

Part Three

Recipes for the Table

Are you hungry? Because it's time to eat. Luckily, with the help of the food processor, you won't have to spend hours in the kitchen to get fresh, wholesome meals on the table any time of day. I'll show you how to whip up the fluffiest scones, muffins that masquerade as pumpkin pie (but are actually healthy), crunchy granola clusters, and buttermilk biscuits that my Southern husband adores—and that's just breakfast. From there we'll knock out some of my family's favorite soups, salads, and sides, as well as main courses that will appease every eater in the bunch. From Black Bean Veggie Burgers (page 206) that even my picky five-year-old will devour, to crowd-pleasing Chicken and Peach Kebabs with Peanut Dipping Sauce (page 174), to my husband's favorite sticky Sriracha Chicken Wings (page 168), and a Crispy Maple-Walnut–Crusted Salmon (page 160) that looks darn impressive but comes together in minutes, these are recipes you can come back to again and again. So, gather your friends and family, and, as we say in my house before every meal, *cheers!*

Breakfasts & Baked Goods

Pumpkin-Almond Muffins

Prep time: 15 minutes • Cook time: 35 minutes

GLUTEN-FREE, VEGETARIAN

These are my five-year-old's favorite muffins. Mine too. They're tender and moist, with a light, melt-in-your-mouth crumb and a flavor that sings of pumpkin pie. As opposed to the overly sweet-ened "cakes" that often disguise themselves as breakfast muffins, these nutritious beauties are sweetened with a touch of honey and made with almond and coconut flour, giving them a healthy boost of protein. MAKES 8 MUFFINS

¾ cup pumpkin purée or canned pumpkin

⅓ cup honey

2 tablespoons extra-virgin coconut oil, melted

1 teaspoon ground cinnamon

½ teaspoon ground nutmeg

¼ teaspoon ground ginger

Pinch ground cloves

¼ teaspoon kosher salt

2 large eggs

1½ cups almond flour

1 tablespoon coconut flour

½ teaspoon baking soda

STORAGE The muffins can be stored in an airtight container at room temperature or in the refrigerator for up to 3 days. They can also be frozen for up to 2 months.

1. Preheat the oven to 350°F. Line the cups of an 8-muffin tin with paper liners.

2. Fit the food processor with the *s blade*. Add the pumpkin, honey, coconut oil, cinna-mon, nutmeg, ginger, cloves, and salt. Process until smooth. Stop and scrape down the sides. Add the eggs, and process for 10 seconds.

3. In a medium bowl, mix together the almond flour, coconut flour, and baking soda. Sprinkle the dry mixture evenly over the wet ingredients in the processor. Pulse until combined and no lumps remain.

4. Using a rubber spatula, scrape the blade clean. Wipe down the sides of the work bowl, and stir gently to incorporate any streaks of flour.

5. Divide the batter evenly among the muffin cups. Bake for 30 to 35 minutes, turning the pan 180 degrees halfway through. Bake until the muffins are golden brown and a toothpick inserted in the center comes out clean. Let cool in the pan for 5 minutes, then transfer to a wire rack and cool com-pletely before serving.

Creamy Buckwheat Power Bowls

Prep time: 5 minutes, plus 8 hours to soak

GLUTEN-FREE, NUT-FREE OPTION, VEGAN OPTION

Buck-what? Buckwheat is a highly nutritious and naturally gluten-free seed that you can find at most grocery stores—just don't buy kasha, the toasted version, for this recipe. After buckwheat soaks in water overnight, it gets buzzed in the food processor with cinnamon, milk, and maple syrup until it's smooth, creamy, and sweet. It then gets topped with your favorite fixings, from fresh berries to roasted nuts. I usually make it ahead of time and store it in to-go containers for a grab-and-go breakfast that's way healthier and tastier than those packaged energy bars. SERVES 2

1 cup raw buckwheat groats

⅛ teaspoon kosher salt

¼ teaspoon ground cinnamon

¼ cup dairy milk (for the nut-free version), nut milk (for the vegan version), or coconut milk (for a nut-free and vegan version), plus more for serving

Maple syrup or stevia to sweeten (or honey if not vegan)

Optional toppings: berries, flax seeds, chia seeds, roasted chopped nuts, toasted coconut flakes

STORAGE The buckwheat can be refrigerated for up to 3 days.

TIME SAVER I like to make the buckwheat ahead of time and divide it between two to-go containers for a quick grab-and-go breakfast.

1. In a medium bowl, cover the buckwheat with an inch or two of lukewarm water. Let sit at room temperature for at least 8 hours or overnight.

2. Fit the food processor with the *s blade*. Drain the buckwheat, and rinse well. Transfer to the food processor along with the salt and cinnamon. Process until coarsely ground. Stop and scrape down the sides.

3. Add the milk, and process until smooth. Add the sweetener. Pulse to combine. Season with additional salt as needed.

4. Transfer the buckwheat to 2 bowls, add the toppings of your choice, and serve. If you'd like, finish with a drizzle of milk.

Grandma's Banana Bread

Prep time: 10 minutes • Cook time: 50 minutes

NUT-FREE, VEGETARIAN

This was my grandma's recipe, and it's the best banana bread in the world. Okay, I might be slightly biased, but seriously, it's the best. It's super moist, and if you're able to hold out, it forms an irresistible sticky-sweet crust after a day. My grandma made hers by hand, but I've adapted the recipe using the food processor, which makes it super easy and quick. The bread doesn't need any extras (after all, it doesn't exactly skimp on butter or sugar), but if you serve the slices with a smear of good-quality butter and a sprinkle of flaky sea salt, your family and friends will bow at your feet. MAKES 2 (8½-BY-4½-INCH OR 9-BY-4-INCH) LOAVES

1 stick unsalted butter, at room temperature, plus more for greasing

3 very ripe large bananas, peeled

1¼ cups sugar

2 eggs

2 cups all-purpose flour

1 teaspoon baking soda

¼ teaspoon kosher salt

1. Preheat the oven to 350°F. Grease 2 (8½-by-4½-inch) or (9-by-4-inch) loaf pans with butter.

2. Fit the food processor with the *s blade*. Break the bananas in half, and put them in the processor. Process until almost smooth, but with some chunks remaining.

3. Add the butter and sugar. Process until smooth. Add the eggs, and process until fully incorporated, about 5 to 8 seconds.

4. Sprinkle the flour, baking soda, and salt evenly over the top of the banana mixture. Pulse just until the flour is incorporated, about 10 pulses. It's okay if you still see streaks of white—don't overmix.

5. Using a rubber spatula, scrape the blade clean. Wipe down the sides of the work bowl, and stir gently to incorporate any streaks of flour.

6. Divide the batter between the prepared loaf pans, and smooth the tops. Bake for 45 to 50 minutes, until the loaves are browned and a toothpick inserted in the center comes out clean. Cool for 5 minutes in the pan. Run a knife along the edges, then invert the pans to remove the loaves. Cool, right-side up, on a wire rack, and serve.

STORAGE The banana bread is even better the next day, if you can wait that long! It will keep for up to 1 week tightly wrapped at room temperature, or even longer in the refrigerator. It can also be frozen for up to 2 months.

TIME SAVER It's important for the butter to be at room temperature in this recipe so that it fully incorporates into the batter. But what if you forget to take it out of the fridge early enough (or, like me, you often take up baking projects at the last minute)? To soften butter quickly, cut it into small chunks and place it on a plate or in a bowl on top of the stove while the oven preheats. If my kitchen is warm enough, the butter will usually be soft by the time I'm ready for it. If the butter is still cold, place it in the microwave on defrost for 5- to 10-second bursts, until it's softened but not melted.

Whole-Wheat
Zucchini Muffins

Prep time: 20 minutes • Cook time: 35 minutes

NUT-FREE, VEGAN

Homemade muffins without dirtying a single bowl? That's right; these delicious and nutritious muffins get made right in the food processor. Made with whole-wheat pastry flour, maple syrup, and flax seeds in place of eggs (making them vegan), these healthy bites are perfect for breakfast, lunch boxes, and afternoon snacks. They taste even better the next day, if you can wait that long. MAKES 12 MUFFINS

¼ cup ground flax seeds

½ medium zucchini (about 4 ounces), trimmed

¼ cup grapeseed, safflower, or canola oil

½ cup plus 1 tablespoon maple syrup

¾ cup nut milk (for a vegan version) or dairy milk (for a nut-free version)

1 teaspoon vanilla extract

1⅓ cups whole-wheat pastry flour

1 teaspoon baking soda

1 teaspoon ground cinnamon

¼ teaspoon kosher salt

⅓ cup chopped toasted walnuts or pecans (optional) (if not nut-free) (see How-to, page 37)

1. Preheat the oven to 350°F. Line the cups of a 12-muffin tin with paper liners.

2. Mix the flax seeds with ¼ cup water, and set aside.

3. Fit the food processor with the *shredding disc*. Push the zucchini through the feed tube to shred. Transfer to a small bowl.

4. Reassemble the food processor with the *s blade* (no need to wash). Add the grapeseed oil, maple syrup, milk, vanilla, and flax seeds (which should now have thickened and absorbed all the water). Process until smooth, about 30 to 60 seconds.

5. Sprinkle the flour, baking soda, cinnamon, and salt evenly over the top of the wet ingredients in the food processor. Pulse 5 times, or until the ingredients are just incorporated. It's okay if there are still streaks of white—don't overmix.

6. Add the shredded zucchini and walnuts (if using), and pulse 2 or 3 times, just to distribute—again, don't overmix.

7. Using a rubber spatula, scrape the blade clean. Wipe down the sides of the work bowl, and stir gently to incorporate any streaks of flour.

8. Divide the batter evenly among the muffin cups. Bake for 30 to 35 minutes, turning the pan 180 degrees halfway through, until the muffins are lightly golden on top and bounce back when gently pressed. Cool the muffins in the pan set on a wire rack, and serve.

STORAGE The muffins can be stored in an airtight container at room temperature or in the refrigerator for up to 3 days (they'll have a slightly denser texture if refrigerated). They can also be frozen for up to 2 months.

HOW-TO The easiest way to divide the muffin batter into cups is to use an ice cream scoop with a lever. That way you get the exact same amount of batter in each cup, and, best of all, there's no drippy mess!

Granola Clusters

Prep time: 15 minutes • Cook time: 45 minutes

GLUTEN-FREE OPTION, VEGETARIAN

We eat a lot of granola in my house. It's a favorite for quick breakfasts and afternoon snacks. For years I made a version that we all liked, but when I started to experiment using the food processor, everything changed. Suddenly, we had clusters—*big, crunchy clusters that not only hold up well in milk but also make for perfect school snacks (or after-lunch treats).* MAKES ABOUT 7 CUPS

1½ cups old-fashioned rolled oats (regular or gluten-free), divided

1 cup pecans

½ cup walnuts

½ cup pumpkin seeds

½ cup coarsely chopped dried fruit such as apricots, dates, cranberries, currants, and cherries

½ cup unsweetened shredded coconut

1 teaspoon ground cinnamon

½ teaspoon kosher salt

⅓ cup honey

¼ cup extra-virgin coconut oil, melted

2 teaspoons vanilla extract

STORAGE The granola clusters can be stored in an airtight container at room temperature for up to 1 week. The granola will soften slightly after a couple of days, but it will still taste delicious.

1. Preheat the oven to 300°F. Line a large baking sheet with parchment paper.

2. Fit the food processor with the *s blade*. Add ½ cup of rolled oats and process to a coarse flour. Add the remaining 1 cup of oats, along with the pecans, walnuts, pumpkin seeds, dried fruit, coconut, cinnamon, and salt. Pulse until the nuts are very coarsely chopped, about 5 to 6 pulses.

3. In a small bowl, stir together the honey, coconut oil, and vanilla. Pour the honey mixture over the ingredients in the food processor, and pulse until the mixture comes together and looks damp, about 8 pulses.

4. Transfer the granola to the baking sheet. Using a rubber spatula, press it into a ½-inch-thick rectangle, about 8-by-12 inches.

5. Bake for 20 minutes. Turn the pan 180 degrees, and bake another 20 to 25 minutes, or until golden brown along the edges and golden on top.

6. Cool the granola on the pan. Break it into clusters before serving.

THE FOOD PROCESSOR FAMILY COOKBOOK

Giant Potato Latke

Prep time: 15 minutes • Cook time: 35 minutes

GLUTEN-FREE, NUT-FREE, VEGETARIAN

Let me start by saying that I had really and truly intended on making individual latkes. Once I started testing this recipe, however, my then-eight-month-old started teething, which meant non-stop screaming. The idea of standing at the stove top, tending batch after batch of frying latkes, seemed impossible. So instead of making a batch of small latkes, I made one giant potato pancake. It turned out to be fabulous. It's crispy on the outside, soft in the middle, and totally easy to make. I cut the latke into wedges, and we devoured it with the traditional accompaniments of applesauce and sour cream. You'll need a 12-inch nonstick skillet with a lid for this recipe. SERVES 6

2 medium russet potatoes (about 1 pound), peeled

½ medium onion, finely chopped

1 egg, beaten

Kosher salt

Freshly ground black pepper

¼ cup plus 1 tablespoon extra-virgin olive oil, divided

Applesauce, for serving (optional)

Sour cream, for serving (optional)

1. Fit the food processor with the *shredding disc*. Push the potatoes through the feed tube to shred.

2. Spread the shredded potatoes out on a clean kitchen towel. Roll it up, and twist and squeeze the towel over the sink to remove as much liquid as possible.

3. Transfer the potatoes to a bowl, and add the onion and beaten egg. Season generously with salt and pepper. Toss to coat.

4. In a 12-inch nonstick skillet over medium heat, heat ¼ cup of olive oil. When the oil is hot, add the potato mixture and press into an even, smooth layer. Reduce the heat to medium low, cover, and let cook until the potatoes are golden on the bottom and tender in the middle, about 15 to 20 minutes. Increase the heat to medium and cook, uncovered, until the latke is nicely browned on the bottom and moves around easily when the pan is shaken, 2 to 5 minutes longer (slide a thin spatula under the latke to loosen, if needed).

5. Slide the latke out onto a plate. Place another plate on top, and flip the latke onto the second plate, so that the cooked side is now on top.

6. Place the pan back over medium heat, and add the remaining tablespoon of olive oil. When hot, slide the latke back into the pan, cooked-side up.

7. Cook over medium heat, uncovered, until the bottom is browned, about 6 to 8 minutes.

8. Slide the latke onto a cutting board, and season with salt. Cut into wedges, and serve with the toppings of your choice or alongside eggs.

TIME SAVER I often make this ahead of time, so that I'm not worried about tending the stove if guests are coming over or stressing about whether the eggs will be ready at the same time. While the latke is cooking, preheat the oven to 200°F and line a baking sheet with parchment paper. Once the latke is cooked, transfer it to the baking sheet and pop it in the oven to keep warm. It can stay in there for up to 30 minutes, although I've been known to leave it longer.

Buttermilk Biscuits

Prep time: 15 minutes • Cook time: 15 minutes

NUT-FREE, VEGETARIAN

These fluffy, flaky biscuits are ridiculously easy to pull together, which means my biscuit-loving, Atlanta-born-and-raised husband gets homemade biscuits once a week—and sometimes more. The ingredients are all pulsed together in the food processor. Use a light touch, pulsing just until the dough comes together, since overworking toughens the biscuits. We eat these beauties alongside eggs or slathered with butter and jam for breakfast. They also make for lovely little ham sandwiches, which are perfect for parties. MAKES 12 (2½-INCH) BISCUITS

2 cups all-purpose flour, plus more for flouring

1 tablespoon baking powder

¼ teaspoon baking soda

1 teaspoon kosher salt

6 tablespoons cold unsalted butter, cut into ½-inch pieces

¾ cup buttermilk

¼ cup heavy (whipping) cream

1 egg, beaten

1. Preheat the oven to 400°F. Line a baking sheet with parchment paper.

2. Fit the food processor with the s *blade*. Add the flour, baking powder, baking soda, and salt. Pulse to combine. Add the cold butter, and pulse 5 to 6 times, just until the butter is cut into pea-size pieces. Drizzle in the buttermilk and heavy cream, and pulse 5 to 6 more times, just until the mixture holds together when pressed. Small balls of butter are okay throughout at this point— don't overwork.

3. On a floured surface, turn out the dough. Using lightly floured hands, form the dough into a ½-inch rectangle, pressing it gently to bring it together. Fold the dough in half like a book and press into another ½-inch rectangle. Fold it again, and pat it again into a ½-inch rectangle. Do this one more time. Using a round biscuit cutter, press down (without twisting) to cut out the biscuits, cutting them as close together as possible. Gather the remaining dough, pat it down, and cut out more biscuits. After that, discard any remaining scraps. Place the biscuits on the parchment-lined baking sheet, and brush the top of each with the beaten egg. Bake until golden, about 15 minutes. Transfer to a wire rack. Serve warm or at room temperature.

STORAGE Biscuits are best the day they're made, but my family still gobbles them up the next day. Store them in an airtight container at room temperature for up to 2 days.

HOW-TO Although it might seem like a strange step to fold the dough several times, this is going to help create layers inside the biscuits, making them flaky and fluffy.

Apricot-Walnut Scones with Honey-Butter Glaze

Prep time: 15 minutes • Cook time: 20 minutes

VEGETARIAN

My friend Annie is a trained pastry chef who, although she has moved on to other things, still bakes amazing treats. Several years ago she taught me how to make scones, and now I make them whenever we have guests. Pulling warm scones out of the oven makes me look like a domestic master, and no one has to know the truth, which is that I hate making pancakes. These scones are so much easier than tending a batch of flapjacks, and they can even be made in advance and frozen for last-minute guests. MAKES 8 SCONES

9 tablespoons cold unsalted butter, divided

½ cup half-and-half

⅓ cup plus 2 tablespoons honey, divided

1 large egg

2¼ cups all-purpose flour, plus more for flouring

1 tablespoon baking powder

½ teaspoon kosher salt

⅓ cup packed finely chopped dried apricots

⅓ cup chopped toasted walnuts (see How-to, page 37)

SIMPLE SWAP Feel free to experiment with your favorite dried fruits and nuts. Cranberries, dates, cherries, and currants are all delicious, as are almonds and pecans. For a nut-free version, simply omit the nuts.

1. Preheat the oven to 400°F. Line a baking sheet with parchment paper.

2. Cut 7 tablespoons of the cold butter into ½-inch cubes, and place it in the refrigerator while you prep the other ingredients. Cold butter is key!

3. In a small bowl, whisk together the half-and-half, ⅓ cup of honey, and the egg.

4. Fit the food processor with the *s blade*. Add the flour, baking powder, and salt. Pulse to combine.

5. Sprinkle the refrigerated butter over the flour, and pulse until the butter is cut into pea-size pieces, about 15 pulses. Add the dried apricots and toasted walnuts. Pulse to incorporate, 2 or 3 pulses.

6. Remove the lid, and pour in the liquid mixture. Pulse just until everything comes together and looks mostly incorporated—you will still see streaks of flour—about 8 to 10 pulses. Don't overwork.

7. Scrape the dough onto the parchment-lined baking sheet. Using floured hands, gently press it into a ½-inch-thick disc, about 8½ to 9 inches wide. Using a floured pastry cutter or knife, cut the dough into 8 wedges (don't separate the wedges). Bake for 18 to 20 minutes, or until golden brown and slightly firm to the touch.

8. While the scones bake, make the glaze. In a small microwavable bowl, combine the remaining 2 tablespoons of butter and the remaining 2 tablespoons of honey, and melt in the microwave or in a small pot on the stove top. When the scones come out of the oven, immediately brush them generously with the glaze (you should use up most of the glaze). Set the pan on a rack to cool.

9. Cut the scones into 8 wedges, and serve warm or at room temperature.

STORAGE The scones can be stored at room temperature for up to 1 day or frozen for up to 2 months. Defrost in a low oven or toaster oven.

Snacks & Sides

Bruschetta with Whipped Goat Cheese

Prep time: 20 minutes, plus 1 hour to sit • Cook time: 10 minutes

NUT-FREE, VEGETARIAN

During a visit to see my family last summer, my brother and his wife made a version of this bruschetta as an appetizer for a Fourth of July barbecue. I loved the twist of spreading toasted crostini with a layer of whipped goat cheese before adding the garlicky tomato and basil mixture. I know it seems as if there are a lot of parts to this recipe, but it all comes together quickly. Warning: These will disappear fast! SERVES 6 TO 8

FOR THE GOAT CHEESE SPREAD

8 ounces goat cheese

3 tablespoons milk

1 tablespoon finely chopped fresh basil

1 tablespoon finely chopped fresh chives

Kosher salt

Freshly ground black pepper

FOR THE CROSTINI

1 baguette, cut into ½-inch slices

¼ cup extra-virgin olive oil

Kosher salt

Freshly ground black pepper

1 garlic clove, peeled and halved

FOR THE TOMATOES

1 large garlic clove, peeled

5 plum tomatoes (about 1 pound), seeded and coarsely chopped

¼ cup lightly packed fresh basil leaves, coarsely chopped

Kosher salt

Freshly ground black pepper

2 teaspoons extra-virgin olive oil

1 teaspoon balsamic vinegar

Flaky sea salt, for serving (optional)

TO MAKE THE GOAT CHEESE SPREAD

1. Fit the mini food processor with the *s blade*. Add the goat cheese and milk. Process until smooth. Stop and scrape down the sides.

2. Add the basil and chives, and season with salt and pepper. Process until smooth. Transfer to a small bowl and leave at room temperature for up to 1 hour, or refrigerate for up to 1 day.

SIMPLE SWAP This bruschetta is also delicious without the goat cheese spread, if you prefer to make these dairy-free. You can also go gluten-free by swapping the bread for a gluten-free baguette.

TO MAKE THE CROSTINI

1. Preheat the oven to 375°F.

2. Arrange the bread slices on a large baking sheet in a single layer. Brush on both sides with the olive oil, and season with salt and pepper. Bake for 5 to 8 minutes, or until lightly crisp on the bottom. Flip and cook an additional 5 to 8 minutes, or until toasted on the other side.

3. Remove the pan from the oven, and immediately rub each crostini with a cut side of the garlic clove. Cool, and let sit at room temperature until ready to use, up to 3 hours.

TO MAKE THE TOMATOES

1. Fit the food processor (standard size) with the *s blade*. With the motor running, drop the garlic clove through the feed tube and finely chop.

2. Add the tomatoes and basil, and season with salt and pepper. Pulse until finely chopped, 10 to 15 pulses. Scrape the mixture into a strainer to drain off any excess liquid.

3. Transfer the mixture to a bowl, and stir in the olive oil and balsamic vinegar. Season with salt and pepper.

4. To assemble the bruschetta, smear each crostini with some of the goat cheese spread. Using a slotted spoon, top each crostini with the tomato mixture. Sprinkle with flaky sea salt (if using), and serve.

Cheddar Wafers

Prep time: 10 minutes, plus 1 hour to chill • Cook time: 20 minutes

NUT-FREE, VEGETARIAN

These crispy, savory cheese wafers are the perfect nibble with a cocktail or glass of wine. My five-year-old says they also go well with a cup of juice. Serve the wafers as an elegant hors d'oeuvre or as an after-school snack. Either way, they're sure to disappear fast. The wafers can be made ahead of time and frozen—perfect for unexpected guests. MAKES ABOUT 30 WAFERS

8 ounces sharp Cheddar cheese

1 stick unsalted butter, at
    room temperature

1 cup all-purpose flour

1 teaspoon salt

Pinch ground cayenne pepper

2 teaspoons water

HOW-TO When shredding cheese using the food processor, cold cheese works best. I find that Cheddar straight out of the refrigerator shreds just fine, but you can also pop it in the freezer for 5 to 10 minutes for added insurance.

1. Fit the food processor with the *shredding disc*. Push the cheese through the feed tube to shred. Transfer to a bowl.

2. Refit the processor with the *s blade* (no need to wash). Add the butter, and process until smooth. Stop and scrape down the sides.

3. Add the shredded cheese, and pulse to combine, about 8 pulses. Stop and scrape down the sides.

4. In a small bowl, stir together the flour, salt, and cayenne. Sprinkle the dry ingredients evenly over the butter mixture in the processor. Pulse until the flour is incorporated and the mixture looks crumbly, about 10 pulses.

5. Drizzle in the water, and pulse 10 times, until the mixture holds together when pressed between your fingers.

6. Transfer the dough to a large piece of plastic wrap, and shape it into a 9- to 10-inch log. Wrap with the plastic wrap, and refrigerate for 1 hour, or up to 48 hours.

7. Preheat the oven to 350°F. Line a baking sheet with parchment paper.

8. Slice the dough into ¼-inch-thick wafers, and line them up on the prepared baking sheet, spacing them 2 inches apart. Bake on the middle rack for 16 to 18 minutes, turning the pan 180 degrees halfway through, or until golden around the edges. Let cool on the pan for 5 minutes, then transfer to a cooling rack and cool completely before serving.

STORAGE The wafers can be stored in an airtight container for up to 2 days or frozen for up to 1 month. Defrost at room temperature or in a low oven before serving.

Cherry-Chocolate Granola Bars

Prep time: 15 minutes, plus 30 minutes to chill • Cook time: 25 minutes

GLUTEN-FREE OPTION, VEGETARIAN

While I pretend to make these chewy, chocolate-studded granola bars for my daughter, I actually make them for myself—they've gotten me through many a tough workday. They're filled with good-for-you ingredients (none of the artificial stuff, thank you very much!), and they come together in under 15 minutes in the food processor. The recipe was inspired by a version by Deb Perelman, author of the food blog Smitten Kitchen. MAKES 12 BARS

Extra-virgin olive oil or cooking spray, for greasing

1½ cups old-fashioned rolled oats (regular or gluten-free), divided

¼ cup peanut or almond butter

¼ cup extra-virgin coconut oil, melted

¼ cup maple syrup

½ teaspoon ground cinnamon

½ teaspoon vanilla extract

¼ teaspoon almond extract

½ teaspoon kosher salt

¾ cup unsweetened shredded coconut

¼ cup hemp seeds

¾ cup dried cherries or cranberries (or any chopped dried fruit)

¾ cup chopped chocolate or chocolate chips

1. Preheat the oven to 350°F. Line an 8-by-8-inch baking dish with a large piece of aluminum foil, leaving an over-hang (you'll use the overhang as handles to pull the bars out later). Brush lightly with olive oil.

2. Fit the food processor with the *s blade*. Add ¼ cup of rolled oats, and process to a fine flour. Transfer the oat flour to a small bowl.

3. Refit the processor with the *s blade* (no need to wash). Add the peanut butter, coconut oil, maple syrup, cinnamon, vanilla extract, almond extract, and salt. Process until smooth.

4. Add the shredded coconut, hemp seeds, ground oat flour, and the remaining 1¼ cups oats. Pulse 10 to 12 times, or until the mixture comes together and looks sticky. Stop and scrape down the sides.

5. Add the dried fruit and the chocolate. Pulse 10 to 12 times, or until the fruit and chocolate are distributed.

6. Transfer the mixture to the prepared baking dish, and press it into a smooth layer, making sure to get it into the corners. Bake for 25 to 30 minutes, or until golden brown along the edges and light golden in the middle. Place the pan on a wire rack, and let cool for 10 minutes. Put the pan in the refrigerator to cool completely before cutting (this makes cutting easier), about 30 minutes.

7. Gripping the foil, lift the bars from the pan. Using a sharp knife, cut into 4-by-1¼-inch rectangles (or whatever size you prefer), and serve.

STORAGE The bars can be stored in an airtight container at room temperature for up to 1 week or frozen for up to 2 months. I like to wrap each bar individually in plastic wrap before freezing.

TIME SAVER These are great make-ahead school or work snacks. I individually wrap the granola bars and store them in a large zip-top bag in my freezer. In the morning before school, I pop one out and put it in my daughter's backpack, or in my purse. By snack time, the bar is defrosted and ready for eating.

Zucchini Cakes

Prep time: 15 minutes • Cook time: 20 minutes

GLUTEN-FREE, VEGETARIAN

When my oldest daughter was a baby, I started making her little vegetable cakes to eat as finger food. They were so good that I often found myself swiping them from her plate when she wasn't looking. Eventually I started feeling guilty about stealing her food, so I started making larger batches for the whole family. While these cakes make a great side dish, I also love serving them as an appetizer with a small dollop of yogurt or sour cream and a sprinkle of fresh basil. MAKES ABOUT 15 TO 20 CAKES

2 medium zucchini (about 1 pound), trimmed

2 eggs, beaten

2 scallions, thinly sliced

¼ cup grated Parmesan cheese

Pinch freshly grated nutmeg

¼ cup almond flour

Salt

Freshly ground black pepper

2 to 3 tablespoons extra-virgin olive oil

Yogurt or sour cream, for serving (optional)

Thinly sliced fresh basil, for serving (optional)

1. Preheat the oven to 200°F. Line a plate with paper towels, and line a baking sheet with parchment paper.

2. Fit the food processor with the *shredding disc*. Push the zucchini through the feed tube to shred. Spread the shredded zucchini out on a clean kitchen towel. Roll it up, and twist and squeeze the towel over the sink to remove as much liquid as possible.

3. Transfer the zucchini to a large bowl, and add the eggs, scallions, Parmesan, nutmeg, and almond flour. Season with salt and pepper, and stir well.

4. In a large nonstick or cast iron skillet over medium-high heat, heat 2 tablespoons of olive oil. Working in batches, drop in spoonfuls (about 2 tablespoons) of the zucchini mixture, flattening the zucchini mounds with the back of the spoon. Be careful not to overcrowd the pan, as this could prevent browning. Cook the cakes until browned on the bottom, about 3 minutes. Flip and cook for an additional 2 to 3 minutes, until browned. Transfer the cakes to the paper towel-lined plate to drain briefly, then pop them onto the parchment-lined baking sheet. Season with a bit more salt, and put the pan in the oven to keep warm.

5. Repeat with the remaining batter, adding more oil to the pan if needed.

6. Serve the cakes on their own or with a dollop of yogurt or sour cream and a sprinkle of fresh basil, if you wish.

SIMPLE SWAP Try swapping out the zucchini for other vegetables, such as summer squash or sweet potatoes.

Cauliflower Purée

Prep time: 10 minutes • Cook time: 15 minutes

GLUTEN-FREE, NUT-FREE, VEGETARIAN

I try not to lie to my kids, but my daughter calls these mashed potatoes, and I don't correct her. Let's just call it an omission of facts. While I can't get her to eat roasted, steamed, or raw cauliflower, she gobbles this up. The creamy and healthy purée often stands in for mashed potatoes at our house, sometimes as a bed for meat and fish. You won't taste the lemon in this recipe, but it will brighten the flavor. SERVES 4

1 large head cauliflower (about 2 pounds), cored, leaves trimmed, and cut into florets

1 large garlic clove, peeled and smashed

1 small bay leaf

2 cups milk

Kosher salt

2 tablespoons butter

Freshly ground black pepper

Lemon wedge

STORAGE The purée can be refrigerated for up to 1 day. Reheat gently before serving. If needed, add a splash or two of water to thin.

SIMPLE SWAP For a vegan version, use vegetable broth instead of milk and swap extra-virgin olive oil for butter.

1. In a medium saucepan, place the cauliflower florets, garlic, bay leaf, and milk (the milk won't cover the cauliflower). Season with salt. Stir, making sure that the garlic and bay leaf are immersed. Bring to a boil over high heat. Reduce the heat to a simmer. Cover and cook, stirring occasionally, until the florets are very tender when pierced with a knife, 10 to 15 minutes.

2. Fit the food processor with the *s blade*. Discard the bay leaf. Using a slotted spoon, transfer the florets and garlic to the processor. Reserve the cooking liquid. Add the butter to the cauliflower, and process until smooth. Stop and scrape down the sides.

3. Add 2 to 4 tablespoons of the cooking liquid. Process until smooth and creamy. You can add more cooking liquid if you prefer a thinner purée. Season with salt, pepper, and a few drops of lemon juice. Serve warm.

Minty Mashed Peas

Prep time: 5 minutes • Cook time: 3 minutes

GLUTEN-FREE, NUT-FREE, VEGETARIAN

If I had been served these as a kid, my relationship with peas would have been much different. I didn't come around to the little green legumes until my twenties, scarred by memories of the flavorless gray peas served in my elementary school cafeteria. I eventually discovered how delicious peas can be when prepared correctly (not boiled to death), and now both of my girls love them. Try this dish with the Marinated Lamb Chops with Mint Pesto (page 186). SERVES 4

1 small garlic clove, peeled

Kosher salt

1 pound fresh or frozen peas

2 tablespoons butter

2 tablespoons coarsely chopped fresh mint

Juice of ½ lemon

Freshly ground black pepper

STORAGE The peas are delicious as leftovers the next day. Cover and store in the refrigerator.

SIMPLE SWAP For a vegan version, swap extra-virgin olive oil for the butter.

1. Fit the food processor with the *s blade*. With the motor running, drop the garlic clove through the feed tube to chop. Stop and scrape down the sides.

2. Bring a medium pot of water to a boil. Season with salt, add the peas, and cook until they're bright green and tender, 2 to 3 minutes. Drain and immediately transfer the peas to the food processor.

3. Add the butter, mint, and lemon juice, and season with salt and pepper. Process to a coarse purée. Taste, season with additional salt and pepper as needed, and serve immediately.

Easy Sweet Potato Bake

Prep time: 20 minutes • Cook time: 40 minutes

GLUTEN-FREE, NUT-FREE, VEGETARIAN

I teach cooking classes, and several students have told me that this dish transformed their families into sweet potato lovers. It's one of my husband's favorite dinners when paired with a simple green salad, and it's one of my favorite Thanksgiving side dishes, as it can be assembled ahead of time. The mixture gets whipped together in the food processor, producing a luxuriously creamy yet surprisingly light texture—I sometimes call it a soufflé, even though the eggs are not separated. SERVES 6

Butter, for greasing

4 ounces Comté or Gruyère cheese, divided

2 or 3 large sweet potatoes (about 3 pounds), peeled and cut into 1-inch chunks

Kosher salt

6 tablespoons butter, cut into pieces

¼ teaspoon ground cinnamon

⅛ teaspoon ground nutmeg

2 tablespoons brown sugar

½ cup heavy (whipping) cream

Freshly ground black pepper

3 large eggs

1. Preheat the oven to 425°F. Butter a 2-quart casserole dish.

2. Fit the food processor with the *shredding disc*. Push the cheese through the feed tube to shred. Transfer to a bowl, and set aside. Refit the processor with the *s blade* (no need to wash).

3. In a large saucepan over high heat, cover the potatoes with water. Season with salt. Bring to a boil then lower to a simmer and cook until the potatoes are tender, about 9 minutes. Drain and transfer to the food processor. Add the butter, and process until smooth.

4. Add the cinnamon, nutmeg, brown sugar, and heavy cream, and season with salt and pepper. Process until combined. Let the mixture cool slightly.

5. Add the eggs, and process until light and fluffy. Add half of the shredded cheese, and pulse until combined.

6. Transfer the mixture to the prepared casserole dish, and smooth out the top with a spatula. Sprinkle the remaining cheese over the top. Bake for 20 to 25 minutes, or until puffed and golden around the edges, and serve.

TIME SAVER This is a fantastic holiday or special-occasion side dish, as it can be completely assembled in advance before baking. Simply cover the top with plastic wrap, and pop it in the refrigerator for up to 1 day. Bring it to room temperature before baking.

Roasted Smashed Potatoes with Avocado Crema

Prep time: 20 minutes • Cook time: 1 hour

GLUTEN-FREE, NUT-FREE, VEGETARIAN

The inspiration for these crispy potatoes, served with a cool and creamy avocado crema, came from my brother and his wife, who made a version for us last year on vacation. They were so good that we begged them to make them again two days later. The avocado crema is delicious on its own with grilled vegetables, fish, or chicken. Serve the potatoes with anything grilled; I especially love them with the Chipotle-Garlic Grilled Chicken (page 172). SERVES 4 TO 6

FOR THE AVOCADO CREMA

1 garlic clove, peeled

⅓ cup lightly packed fresh basil leaves

1 medium avocado, halved and pitted

⅓ cup sour cream

½ tablespoon freshly squeezed lime juice

Kosher salt

Freshly ground black pepper

FOR THE POTATOES

1 pound baby red or yellow potatoes

Kosher salt

4 tablespoons extra-virgin olive oil, divided

Freshly ground black pepper

TO MAKE THE AVOCADO CREMA

1. Fit the mini food processor with the *s blade*. Add the garlic, and process until finely chopped. Add the basil leaves, and process until finely chopped. Stop and scrape down the sides.

2. Scoop the avocado flesh into the processor, and add the sour cream and lime juice. Season with salt and pepper. Process until smooth, stopping and scraping down the sides occasionally. Taste and season with additional salt and pepper as needed.

3. Transfer to a medium bowl. Cover with plastic wrap, placing the plastic wrap directly on the surface of the crema. Refrigerate until ready to use, up to 2 hours.

TO MAKE THE POTATOES

1. Preheat the oven to 450°F.

2. In a medium saucepan, cover the potatoes with water, and place over high heat. Season generously with salt. Bring to a boil. Cook the potatoes at a gentle boil until tender when pierced with a knife, about 15 to 30 minutes, depending on the size of the potatoes. Drain.

3. Line a large baking sheet with foil, and rub with 2 tablespoons of olive oil. Arrange the potatoes on the baking sheet. Using the bottom of a flat cup or a ramekin, press down on the potatoes to flatten them to a ½-inch thickness. Don't worry if some of the potatoes break. When all the potatoes are flattened, drizzle them with the remaining 2 tablespoons of olive oil. Season with salt and pepper.

4. Roast the potatoes for 30 to 40 minutes, flipping them halfway through, until golden brown and crispy on both sides. Serve warm with a dollop of the avocado crema.

Butternut Squash Purée

Prep time: 10 minutes • Cook time: 45 minutes

GLUTEN-FREE, NUT-FREE, VEGETARIAN

This is one of my very favorite side dishes, especially once the weather starts to cool. In fact, it's an awesome Thanksgiving side dish because it can be made ahead of time and is mostly hands-off. I also love to serve it as a bed for scallops or white fish. For a vegan version, swap out the butter for coconut oil. SERVES 6

Extra-virgin olive oil, for greasing

1 large butternut squash (about 3 pounds)

3 tablespoons butter

½ teaspoon ground cinnamon

Pinch freshly grated nutmeg

1 teaspoon maple syrup

Kosher salt

Freshly ground black pepper

STORAGE The purée can be refrigerated for up to 5 days.

HOW-TO To cut a butternut squash in half lengthwise, first trim off both ends of the squash. Stand it up on one of the flat ends, and then, using both hands, run a large knife down the center.

1. Preheat the oven to 400°F. Line a baking sheet with parchment paper, and drizzle it with olive oil.

2. Trim off both ends of the squash, then halve it lengthwise. Scrape out and discard the seeds. Place the squash halves, cut-side down, on the prepared baking sheet. Bake until very tender, about 45 minutes. Let cool slightly.

3. Fit the food processor with the *s blade*. Scrape the squash flesh into the processor, discarding the skin. Add the butter, cinnamon, nutmeg, and maple syrup, and season with salt and pepper. Process until smooth, stopping and scraping down the sides occasionally. If needed, reheat the purée in a medium saucepan to heat through. Serve warm.

Corn Pudding

Prep time: 15 minutes • Cook time: 25 minutes

GLUTEN-FREE, NUT-FREE, VEGETARIAN

Spoon me up a big plate of this corn pudding, toss a salad alongside, and I'm set for dinner. There's nothing like the flavor of sweet corn in summer, and here it gets puréed with eggs, milk, Parmesan, and cornmeal to create something that I describe as the love child of a pudding, quiche, and cornbread. The texture is smooth and voluptuous, accented by pops of sweet corn, but it holds its shape. Serve this as a side dish to just about anything, or do as I do and make a meal of it. SERVES 4 TO 6

1 garlic clove, peeled

3 cups fresh corn kernels
(from about 3 or 4 ears), divided

3 large eggs

¾ cup whole milk

½ cup grated Parmesan cheese

¼ cup fine cornmeal or corn flour

½ teaspoon sugar

Pinch freshly grated nutmeg

2 scallions, thinly sliced

Kosher salt

Freshly ground black pepper

2 tablespoons butter

INGREDIENT INFO I prefer to use kosher salt, which has a milder flavor and larger crystal size than table salt, which tastes more "salty" and acidic. Since the two have different size crystals, they aren't interchangeable in terms of measuring (1 teaspoon of kosher salt actually contains less salt than 1 teaspoon of table salt). If a recipe doesn't include a measured amount of salt, feel free to use whatever salt you have or prefer.

1. Preheat the oven to 350°F.

2. Fit the food processor with the *s blade*. With the motor running, drop the garlic clove through the feed tube to chop. Add 2 cups of corn, along with the eggs, milk, Parmesan cheese, cornmeal, sugar, and nutmeg. Process until smooth.

3. Add the remaining cup of corn kernels and the scallions, and season with salt and pepper. Pulse 2 or 3 times to combine.

4. In a 10-inch cast iron or ovenproof skillet over high heat, melt the butter and swirl to coat the skillet, then carefully pour the processed mixture into the hot skillet.

5. Transfer the skillet to the oven, and bake until the edges are golden and the middle is set, about 22 to 25 minutes. Let cool for 5 minutes before serving.

Potato Gratin

Prep time: 20 minutes • Cook time: 45 minutes

GLUTEN-FREE, NUT-FREE, VEGETARIAN

While potato gratin might seem like a fussy dish, this recipe makes it totally simple. First of all, the food processor does the hard work of shredding the cheese and slicing the potatoes. You don't even need to clean the work bowl in between. Then, I start the gratin on the stove top—it's a technique I learned in cooking school. The whole thing is then dumped into a baking dish. It's baked until browned, bubbly, and absolutely irresistible. SERVES 6

Butter, for greasing

4 ounces Gruyère or Comté cheese

4 medium Yukon gold potatoes
(about 2 pounds), peeled

1½ cups half-and-half

1 large garlic clove, grated on a microplane

Pinch freshly grated nutmeg

Kosher salt

1. Preheat the oven to 400°F. Butter an 8-by-8-inch baking dish.

2. Fit the food processor with the *shredding disc*. Push the cheese through the feed tube to shred. Transfer to a small bowl.

3. Refit the processor with the *slicing disc* (no need to wash). Push the potatoes through the feed tube to slice.

4. Transfer the potatoes to a medium saucepan. Add the half-and-half, garlic, and nutmeg. Season generously with salt, and stir gently to combine. Bring to a boil over medium-high heat, stirring occasionally. Cook at a gentle boil, stirring with a rubber spatula often, until the half-and-half has reduced and richly coats the potatoes, about 8 minutes.

5. Transfer the mixture to the baking dish, and smooth out the top. Sprinkle the shredded cheese evenly over the potatoes. Bake for 30 to 35 minutes, or until the potatoes are tender when pierced with a knife and the top is golden brown. Let sit for 5 to 10 minutes before serving.

Curried Carrot-Coconut Brown Rice

Prep time: 10 minutes • Cook time: 1 hour

GLUTEN-FREE, NUT-FREE, VEGAN

I call this Jamaica rice. It's a golden mélange of carrots, coconut, and brown rice with a hint of sweetness from curry powder, garam masala, and golden raisins. Serve with the Coffee-Marinated Grilled Pork Tenderloin (page 190), or with seared fish, shrimp, or scallops. SERVES 4 TO 6

1 tablespoon peeled and coarsely chopped fresh ginger

½ medium onion, coarsely chopped

2 medium carrots, trimmed

2 tablespoons extra-virgin coconut oil

Kosher salt

Freshly ground black pepper

¼ cup unsweetened shredded coconut

¼ teaspoon curry powder

¼ teaspoon garam masala

¼ cup golden raisins

1 cup brown basmati rice

2 cups water

1. Fit the food processor with the *s blade.* Add the ginger, and process until finely chopped. Add the onion, and pulse until finely chopped, 15 to 20 pulses, stopping and scraping down the sides halfway through.

2. Leaving the ginger and onion in the work bowl, remove the blade and refit the processor with the *shredding disc.* Push the carrots through the feed tube to shred.

3. In a medium saucepan over medium heat, melt the coconut oil. Scrape in the vegetables from the food processor, and season with salt and pepper. Cook, stirring occasionally, until the vegetables are tender but not browned, about 5 minutes.

4. Add the coconut, curry powder, and garam masala. Cook, stirring, for 30 seconds. Stir in the raisins and rice. Pour in the water, and season with salt and pepper. Bring to a boil. Reduce the heat to low, and cook, covered, for 40 minutes.

5. Check the rice and, if the pan looks dry, add another ¼ cup of water. Cover and cook for 10 minutes longer, or until the rice is tender and the liquid has absorbed. Let sit, covered, for 5 minutes before serving.

7

Soups

Roasted Root Vegetable Soup

Prep time: 20 minutes • Cook time: 50 minutes

GLUTEN-FREE, NUT-FREE OPTION, VEGETARIAN

It gets cold in the Hudson Valley where I live. On cold and snowy nights, this soup is what I want. The vegetables are roasted first, making them caramelized and sweet, then they're puréed in the food processor with broth. Done. SERVES 4 TO 6

8 medium carrots (about 1 pound), trimmed, peeled, and cut into 1-inch pieces

4 medium parsnips (about 1 pound), trimmed, peeled, and cut into 1-inch pieces

1 large sweet potato (about 1 pound), peeled and cut into 1-inch pieces

1 tablespoon fresh thyme leaves

3 tablespoons extra-virgin olive oil

Kosher salt

Freshly ground black pepper

4 cups low-sodium vegetable broth (or chicken broth if not vegetarian), divided

2 cups water

⅛ teaspoon freshly squeezed lemon juice

Crème fraîche or sour cream, for serving (optional)

⅓ cup chopped toasted pecans, for serving (optional) (see How-to, page 37)

STORAGE The soup can be refrigerated for up to 5 days or frozen for up to 2 months. If needed, thin the soup with water before reheating.

1. Preheat the oven to 400°F. Line a large baking sheet with foil, and add the carrots, parsnips, sweet potato, thyme, and olive oil. Season with salt and pepper, and toss well to coat. Spread the vegetables in a single layer (if your baking sheet isn't large enough, use 2 baking sheets), and roast for 20 minutes. Stir, then place the pan back in the oven and roast until the vegetables are very tender and lightly browned, about 20 to 25 minutes more.

2. Fit the food processor with the *s blade*. Transfer the roasted vegetables to the processor, and process until smooth, stopping and scraping down the sides occasionally. Pour in 2 cups of broth, and process again until smooth.

3. Transfer the purée to a saucepan, and add the remaining broth and the water. Season with salt and pepper. Bring the soup to a boil, and reduce to a simmer. Cook for 5 minutes to let the flavors meld. Add the lemon juice, and taste one more time for seasoning.

4. Ladle the soup into bowls, add a dollop of crème fraîche (if using) and a sprinkle of chopped pecans (if using), and serve.

Chilled Avocado Soup

Prep time: 10 minutes, plus 1 hour to chill

GLUTEN-FREE, NUT-FREE, VEGAN

If I'm looking for a healthy and quick make-ahead lunch, this is what I turn to. In the morning (or, if I'm really on top of my game, the night before) I'll buzz together avocado, cucumbers, tomatillos, and herbs until creamy, then toss the soup in the refrigerator, either in bowls or in thermoses to take to work. The soup also makes for a lovely appetizer when poured into little demitasse or shot glasses. SERVES 2 TO 4

1 garlic clove, peeled

1 cup coarsely chopped tomatillos (about 4 or 5 medium)

1 cup coarsely chopped seedless (English) cucumber (about ½ large)

2 scallions, coarsely chopped

1 tablespoon packed fresh mint leaves

1 tablespoon packed fresh basil leaves

1 tablespoon Champagne vinegar

Pinch sugar

¼ cup water

1 medium avocado, halved and pitted

Kosher salt

Freshly ground black pepper

2 tablespoons extra-virgin olive oil, plus more for serving

Flaky sea salt, for serving

Lemon wedges, for serving

STORAGE The soup can be refrigerated for up to 1 day.

SIMPLE SWAP If you can't find tomatillos, you can use green tomatoes instead.

1. Fit the food processor with the *s blade*. With the motor running, drop the garlic clove through the feed tube to chop.

2. Add the tomatillos, cucumber, scallions, mint, basil, vinegar, sugar, and water. Scoop the avocado flesh into the processor, and season with salt and pepper. Process until smooth, stopping and scraping down the sides occasionally.

3. With the motor running, pour the olive oil through the feed tube to incorporate. Taste and season with additional salt and pepper as needed. Transfer the soup to a bowl or pitcher and refrigerate until chilled, at least 1 hour.

4. Divide the soup among 4 small cups or between 2 soup bowls. Drizzle with a bit more olive oil, sprinkle with flaky sea salt, and serve with lemon wedges.

Potato-Leek Soup

Prep time: 20 minutes • Cook time: 30 minutes

GLUTEN-FREE, NUT-FREE, VEGETARIAN

The depth of flavor in this recipe is achieved first by slowly cooking the leeks in butter, then adding potatoes and broth, and finally by finishing with cream and buttermilk (a trick I learned from Kenji López-Alt, author of The Food Lab). *The food processor takes care of all the prep, slicing the leeks and potatoes in mere seconds, as well as puréeing the soup after it simmers.* SERVES 4 TO 6

2 large leeks, white and light green parts only, halved, rinsed, and patted dry

2 tablespoons butter

Kosher salt

2 medium russet potatoes (about 1 pound), peeled

4 cups low-sodium vegetable broth (or chicken broth if not vegetarian)

1 bay leaf

¾ cup heavy (whipping) cream

¼ cup buttermilk

Chopped chives, for serving

1. Fit the food processor with the *slicing disc*. Push the leeks through the feed tube to slice.

2. In a large saucepan over medium heat, melt the butter. Add the leeks, and season with salt. Reduce the heat to medium low and cook, stirring often, until the leeks are tender but not browned, about 10 minutes.

3. In the meantime, reassemble the food processor (no need to wash). Push the potatoes through the feed tube to slice.

4. When the leeks are tender, scrape the potato slices into the pot, and add the broth and bay leaf. Season with salt. Increase the heat to high, and bring to a boil. Reduce to a simmer and cook for 15 minutes, or until the potatoes are very tender. Remove the pot from the heat, and discard the bay leaf. Let cool slightly.

5. Rinse the bowl of the food processor, and refit it with the *s blade*. Carefully transfer half the soup to the food processor. Place a towel over the top to avoid splatters, and process until smooth. Pour the puréed soup through a fine mesh strainer, stirring and pressing with a rubber spatula to work the soup through the strainer.

6. Repeat with the rest of the soup.

7. Add the cream and buttermilk, and season with salt. Return the soup to the pot and reheat over medium low heat. Ladle the soup into bowls, garnish with a sprinkle of chives, and serve.

STORAGE The soup can be refrigerated for up to 3 days.

SIMPLE SWAP Vichyssoise is a creamy potato-leek soup that's typically served chilled. To transform this soup into vichyssoise, simply eat the leftovers straight from the fridge the next day. Or, for a more sophisticated approach, refrigerate the soup before serving. Once chilled, taste it and season with a bit more salt as needed—and don't forget to garnish with chives.

Quick Chilled Cucumber and Yogurt Soup with Dill

Prep time: 10 minutes

GLUTEN-FREE, NUT-FREE, VEGETARIAN

Imagine it's hot out, and you're hungry. You want something cooling and refreshing—and fast. I've got just the thing. This soup couldn't be easier to make, and it requires no advance chilling (although it holds up great if you do want to make it ahead). The trick is to use cold cucumbers and yogurt. This is a rustic soup—the texture won't be perfectly smooth—but that's part of what makes it so good. SERVES 4

1 large garlic clove, peeled

2 large seedless (English) cucumbers (about 2 pounds), coarsely chopped

½ cup plain Greek yogurt (preferably 2% fat)

1 tablespoon freshly squeezed lemon juice

1 tablespoon coarsely chopped fresh dill, plus more for garnish

Kosher salt

Freshly ground black pepper

¼ cup extra-virgin olive oil

Flaky sea salt, for serving (optional)

STORAGE The soup can be refrigerated for up to 1 day.

1. Fit the food processor with the *s blade*. With the motor running, drop the garlic clove through the feed tube to chop.

2. Add the cucumbers, yogurt, lemon juice, and dill, and season with salt and pepper. Process until puréed, stopping and scraping down the sides occasionally.

3. With the motor running, drizzle the olive oil through the feed tube to incorporate. Taste and season well with salt and pepper.

4. Ladle the soup into serving bowls, garnish with chopped dill and flaky sea salt (if using), and serve.

Summer Squash Soup with Pesto

Prep time: 15 minutes • Cook time: 30 minutes

GLUTEN-FREE, VEGETARIAN

While I have a romantic image of myself as a gardener, in reality, I have a brown thumb. My husband is the gardener in the family. He tends our small but bountiful vegetable patch, and I handle the harvest. Every year we end up with an abundance of summer squash, and this is one of my favorite ways to use it up. A drizzle of pesto gives this soup a beautiful color and bright flavor, but leave it out for a nut-free dish. The soup is delicious either warm or chilled. SERVES 4 TO 6

4 tablespoons butter

1 medium onion, thinly sliced

2 medium carrots, trimmed, peeled, and thinly sliced

Salt

4 medium yellow summer squash (about 2 pounds), trimmed, halved lengthwise, and thinly sliced

2 garlic cloves, coarsely chopped

1 medium Yukon gold potato (about ½ pound), peeled, halved, and thinly sliced

4 cups reduced-sodium vegetable broth or water (or chicken broth if not vegetarian)

Freshly ground black pepper

Pesto (page 36), for serving

STORAGE The soup can be refrigerated for up to 5 days or frozen for up to 2 months. If needed, thin with a splash of water before serving.

1. In a large saucepan over medium heat, melt the butter. Add the onion and carrots with a pinch of salt. Cook until softened, stirring occasionally, about 7 minutes.

2. Add the summer squash and garlic. Cook, stirring, for 3 or 4 minutes, or until the garlic is fragrant. Add the potato and the broth, and bring to a boil. Reduce the heat to a simmer and cook, partially covered, until the potatoes and vegetables are very tender, about 15 minutes. Remove from the heat and let cool slightly.

3. Fit the food processor with the *s blade*. Carefully transfer half the soup to the food processor. Place a towel over the top to avoid splatters, and process until smooth. Transfer to a clean pot, and repeat with the second batch.

4. Season with salt and pepper. If you prefer a thinner soup, add a touch more water. Ladle the soup into bowls, and serve with a drizzle of Pesto.

Squash Soup with Coconut and Curry

Prep time: 20 minutes • Cook time: 1½ hours

GLUTEN-FREE, NUT-FREE, VEGAN

Nearly every week I throw together a big pot of soup, usually vegetable-based and puréed until silky. It's one of the only fail-safe methods I have of getting vegetables into my five-year-old. While we all love a classic butternut squash soup, after about the hundredth batch, we were ready for a little change. This soup is a fantastic twist on an old favorite. It's flavored with ginger, curry powder, coconut milk, and a touch of cinnamon and brown sugar. I love to use buttercup squash if I can find it—it has an exceptionally rich flesh—but butternut also works great. SERVES 6

Extra-virgin olive oil, for drizzling

1 large buttercup or butternut squash (about 3½ to 4 pounds)

¼ cup extra-virgin coconut oil (or grapeseed or canola oil)

2 large leeks, white and light green parts only, thinly sliced

2 tablespoons minced fresh ginger

1 serrano chile, seeded and minced

Salt

Freshly ground black pepper

1 tablespoon curry powder

¼ teaspoon ground cinnamon

⅛ teaspoon ground allspice

2 tablespoons brown sugar

1 (13½-ounce) can coconut milk

3 cups water

Juice of ½ lime

1 cup toasted, unsweetened coconut flakes, for serving (see How-to, page 37) (optional)

Fresh cilantro leaves, for serving (optional)

1. Preheat the oven to 400°F. Line a baking sheet with parchment paper, and drizzle it with olive oil.

2. Halve the squash lengthwise, and scrape out and discard the seeds. Place the squash halves, cut-side down, on the prepared baking sheet. Bake until very tender, about 45 minutes. Let cool, then scoop out the flesh (you should have roughly 4 cups).

3. In a large saucepan over medium-low heat, heat the coconut oil. Add the leeks, ginger, and serrano chile, and season with salt and pepper. Cook, stirring occasionally, for 8 to 10 minutes, or until the leeks are tender but not browned.

4. Add the curry powder, cinnamon, and allspice, and cook until fragrant, about 1 minute.

5. Stir in the reserved squash, the brown sugar, and another pinch of salt and pepper. Pour in the coconut milk and water. Stir, breaking up the squash with a wooden spoon. Increase the heat to medium high, cover, and bring to a boil. Reduce the heat to a simmer and cook, covered, for 20 minutes.

6. Fit the food processor with the *s blade*. Carefully transfer half the soup to the processor. Place a towel over the top to avoid splatters, and process until smooth. Transfer to a clean pot, and repeat with the second batch.

7. Squeeze in the lime juice, and season with salt and pepper. Reheat over medium low heat, adding a touch more water if you prefer a thinner soup.

8. Ladle the soup into serving bowls, garnish with toasted coconut and a few cilantro leaves (if using), and serve.

STORAGE The soup can be refrigerated for up to 5 days or frozen for up to 2 months. If needed, thin with a splash of water before serving.

TIME SAVER Looking to get a head start? The squash can be roasted up to 3 days in advance. Scoop out the flesh, and refrigerate until you're ready to use it.

Ruby Red Gazpacho

Prep time: 15 minutes, plus 2 hours to chill

GLUTEN-FREE, NUT-FREE, VEGAN

If you want a taste of summer, this is it. This refreshing gazpacho is one of the best things you'll taste all season. Before serving, I like to drizzle the gazpacho with a bit of good-quality olive oil and sprinkle it with some fresh basil. It makes for a beautiful first course, or a crowd-pleasing main course when paired with grilled cheese sandwiches or paninis. The soup is even better the next day, after the flavors have had plenty of time to meld. SERVES 4 TO 6

2 garlic cloves, peeled

3 large tomatoes (about 2 pounds), preferably heirloom, cored and coarsely chopped

1 cup coarsely chopped seedless (English) cucumber (about ½ large)

1 medium shallot, coarsely chopped

¼ green bell pepper, coarsely chopped

1 cup tomato juice

¼ cup Champagne vinegar

Kosher salt

Freshly ground black pepper

¼ cup extra-virgin olive oil, plus more for serving

2 tablespoons thinly sliced fresh basil

STORAGE The gazpacho can be refrigerated for up to 1 day.

1. Fit the food processor with the s *blade.* With the motor running, drop the garlic through the feed tube to chop. Add the tomatoes, cucumber, shallot, bell pepper, tomato juice, and vinegar, and season with salt and pepper. Process until smooth.

2. With the motor running, drizzle the olive oil through the feed tube to incorporate. Taste and season with salt and pepper as needed.

3. Transfer the gazpacho to a bowl or pitcher, and refrigerate for 2 to 24 hours.

4. Before serving, stir well (it will separate in the fridge). Taste and season with additional salt and pepper as needed. Ladle the gazpacho into bowls, drizzle with a bit more olive oil, and garnish with the thinly sliced basil.

Indian Spiced Chickpea and Collard Greens Stew

Prep time: 15 minutes • Cook time: 25 minutes

GLUTEN-FREE, NUT-FREE, VEGETARIAN

This one-dish stew is my go-to dinner whenever anybody in the family starts to get sick. It's warming, a bit spicy, and has serious healing powers (well, at least I think so!). The trick is to finely chop the onion, garlic, jalapeño, and ginger in the food processor until they form a coarse paste, a powerful base for the stew. At the end, the chutney adds a bit of sweetness and the yogurt cools things down to just the right level. SERVES 4

1 medium red onion, coarsely chopped

4 large garlic cloves, peeled

2 jalapeño peppers, seeded and inner ribs discarded, coarsely chopped

1 tablespoon peeled and coarsely chopped fresh ginger

2 tablespoons grapeseed oil

Kosher salt

Freshly ground black pepper

2 teaspoons garam masala

1 teaspoon ground cumin

1 teaspoon ground coriander

⅛ teaspoon ground cinnamon

1 (15-ounce) can diced tomatoes

2 cups water

2 (15-ounce) cans chickpeas, drained and rinsed

2 cups thinly sliced collard greens, stems discarded

¼ cup dried currants

2 tablespoons coarsely chopped fresh cilantro, plus more for serving

Juice of ½ lime

Cooked basmati rice, for serving

Plain yogurt, for serving

Mango chutney, for serving

1. Fit the food processor with the *s blade*. Add the onion, garlic, jalapeño, and ginger. Process to a coarse paste, stopping and scraping down the sides occasionally.

2. In a large straight-sided skillet over medium heat, heat the grapeseed oil. Scrape in the mixture from the processor, and season with salt and pepper. Cook, stirring often, until the mixture thickens and turns golden (it's okay if the bottom of the pan starts to brown), about 5 minutes.

3. Stir in the garam masala, cumin, coriander, and cinnamon, and cook for 30 seconds. Add the tomatoes with their liquid and the water, chickpeas, and a large pinch of salt. Stir, scraping up any brown bits from the bottom of the pan. Bring to a simmer and cook for 10 minutes, stirring occasionally, or until slightly thickened.

4. Add the collard greens and currants. Cook for 3 to 5 minutes, or until the greens are tender. Remove from the heat, and stir in the chopped cilantro and lime juice. Taste and season with additional salt and pepper as needed. If you have the time, let the stew sit for 10 minutes, or up to an hour, to let the flavors meld.

5. Serve the stew over basmati rice with a dollop of yogurt, a spoonful of mango chutney, and a sprinkle of cilantro.

STORAGE The stew can be refrigerated for up to 3 days.

SIMPLE SWAP I love collard greens in soups and stews (and this is a great time to experiment with them), but you could also use spinach, kale, or Swiss chard. Cut out and discard the thick center stems from all but the spinach before cooking.

Sweet Corn Chowder

Prep time: 10 minutes • Cook time: 30 minutes

GLUTEN-FREE, NUT-FREE, VEGETARIAN

I'm originally from the Midwest, and corn runs in my blood. When July rolls around and fresh corn finally arrives at the farmers' market, we eat as much as we can. This chowder is one of my favorite soups. It's lighter in flavor and texture than traditional chowders, with a sweet flavor that's bolstered by a touch of heat from jalapeño and a hint of smokiness from ground cumin. Warm, butter-smeared corn bread is a delicious accompaniment. SERVES 4 TO 6

5 large ears corn

2 garlic cloves, peeled

1 jalapeño pepper, halved, seeded, and inner ribs discarded

1 medium onion, coarsely chopped

4 tablespoons butter

Kosher salt

1 teaspoon ground cumin

½ teaspoon dried oregano

1 medium Yukon gold potato (½ pound), peeled and chopped

1 large fresh cilantro sprig, plus 2 tablespoons finely chopped for serving

5 cups water

½ cup heavy (whipping) cream

Juice of ¼ lime

1. Cut the corn kernels off the cobs, and measure out 4 cups (save any leftovers for another use). Reserve 4 of the cobs.

2. Fit the food processor with the *s blade*. With the motor running, drop the garlic and jalapeño through the feed tube to chop. Add the onion, and pulse to finely chop, about 15 pulses.

3. In a large saucepan over medium heat, melt the butter. Add the chopped vegetables, season with salt, and add the cumin and oregano. Cook until the onion is softened, stirring occasionally, about 5 minutes.

4. Add the potato, cilantro sprig, corn kernels, and reserved cobs. Pour in the water, and season with salt. Bring to a boil. Reduce the heat to a simmer, and cook for 30 minutes. Remove and discard the cilantro sprig and corn cobs. Let cool slightly.

5. Rinse out the bowl of the food processor, and refit it with the s *blade*. Carefully transfer half the soup to the food processor. Place a towel over the top to avoid splatters, and process until smooth. Transfer to a clean pot, and repeat with the second batch.

6. Stir in the heavy cream, and squeeze in a few drops of lime juice. Season with salt. Reheat over medium-low heat before serving. Ladle the chowder into bowls, and garnish with finely chopped cilantro.

STORAGE The chowder can be refrigerated for up to 2 days.

HOW-TO To cut the kernels off the cobs without having them fly all around the kitchen, place the corn cob in a large bowl. Hold it at a slight angle, and cut off the kernels right into the bowl.

Sweet Potato Soup

Prep time: 15 minutes • Cook time: 25 minutes

GLUTEN-FREE, VEGETARIAN

This is my five-year-old's favorite soup (and probably my nine-month-old's as well, at least from what I can gather from her babbles and grunts). Throw a grilled cheese sandwich on the skillet— Gruyère is especially tasty with the soup—and dinner is done. While the soup is kid-friendly, it's also a wonderful first course for dinners with the grown-ups. SERVES 4 TO 6

3 tablespoons butter

1 large leek, white and light green parts only, rinsed well and thinly sliced

Kosher salt

Freshly ground black pepper

2 large garlic cloves, coarsely chopped

½ teaspoon chopped fresh rosemary

½ teaspoon chopped fresh thyme

1 bay leaf

¼ teaspoon ground cinnamon

Pinch freshly grated nutmeg

⅛ teaspoon ancho chili powder

Pinch ground cayenne pepper

2 large sweet potatoes (about 2 pounds), peeled and cut into 1-inch cubes

5 cups water

⅓ cup chopped toasted pecans, for serving (optional) (see How-to, page 37)

1. In a large saucepan over medium heat, melt the butter. Add the leek, and season with salt and pepper. Cook, stirring occasionally, until softened but not browned, about 3 minutes.

2. Add the garlic, rosemary, thyme, bay leaf, cinnamon, nutmeg, ancho chili powder, and cayenne. Cook, stirring, until fragrant, about 1 minute.

3. Add the sweet potatoes, and season with salt and pepper. Cook, stirring, to coat the sweet potatoes in the spices, 30 seconds.

4. Pour in the water. Bring to a boil then reduce to a simmer and cook, partially covered, until the sweet potatoes are completely tender, about 15 minutes.

5. Remove the bay leaf, and let the soup cool slightly.

6. Fit the food processor with the *s blade*. Carefully transfer the soup to the processor. Place a towel over the top to avoid splatters, and process until smooth. Return the soup to the pot.

7. Taste and season with additional salt and pepper as needed. If you prefer a thinner soup, add a touch more water. Reheat gently before serving. Serve with a sprinkle of chopped pecans, if you'd like.

STORAGE The soup can refrigerated for up to 5 days or frozen for up to 2 months. If needed, thin with a splash of water before serving.

SIMPLE SWAP This soup is not so much a recipe as a technique. You can swap the leek for a sweet onion, and change up the herbs and spices to make it your own. Ginger and curry powder or chili powder and cumin make great pairings in this dish. Simply omit the pecans to make it nut-free.

Hearty Tomato Soup with Cheddar Croutons

Prep time: 10 minutes • Cook time: 30 minutes

NUT-FREE, VEGETARIAN

Warm tomato soup. Crispy Cheddar croutons. Dunk and eat. Repeat. Need I say anything else? This rustic tomato soup is a breeze to pull together. It's hearty and satisfying, and, in a nod to the classic grilled-cheese-and-tomato-soup combo, it's served with quick Cheddar croutons. This is sure to cheer up a gloomy day, even when tomato season is a distant memory. SERVES 4

FOR THE SOUP

2 tablespoons extra-virgin olive oil

1 small onion, chopped

Kosher salt

Freshly ground black pepper

2 garlic cloves, chopped

½ teaspoon chopped fresh thyme

½ teaspoon chopped fresh rosemary

½ teaspoon dried oregano

1 tablespoon tomato paste

2 (28-ounce) cans whole, peeled tomatoes

1½ teaspoons sugar

1 cup low-sodium vegetable broth (or chicken broth if not vegetarian)

1 cup heavy (whipping) cream

FOR THE CROUTONS

8 (½-inch) slices French bread, cut on the diagonal

4 ounces Cheddar cheese

TO MAKE THE SOUP

1. In a medium saucepan over medium heat, heat the olive oil. Add the onion, and season with salt and pepper. Cook, stirring occasionally, until tender, about 7 minutes. Add the garlic, thyme, rosemary, and oregano. Cook, stirring, for 1 minute.

2. Add the tomato paste and cook, stirring, until slightly darkened, about 1 minute. Stir in the tomatoes with their juices and the sugar, and season with salt and pepper. Bring the mixture to a simmer. Cook, stirring occasionally and breaking up the tomatoes with a wooden spoon, for 5 minutes. Let cool slightly.

3. Fit the food processor with the s *blade*. Carefully transfer half the soup to a food processor. Place a towel over the top to avoid splatters, and process until smooth. Transfer to a clean pot, and repeat with the second batch.

4. Stir in the broth and heavy cream. Bring to a simmer, and let cook for 5 to 10 minutes. Taste and add additional salt, pepper, or sugar as needed.

STORAGE The soup, without the croutons, can be refrigerated for up to 3 days.

HOW-TO By cooking the bread on a wire rack, you allow air to circulate underneath it, letting the bottom get crispy without the need for oil.

TO MAKE THE CROUTONS

1. Preheat the oven to 375°F. Line a large baking sheet with aluminum foil, and place a metal rack on top. Arrange the slices of bread on the rack in a single layer.

2. Fit the food processor with the *shredding disc*. Push the cheese through the feed tube to shred. Divide the cheese over the tops of the bread. Bake for 7 to 10 minutes, or until the cheese is melted and golden and the bread is crisp.

3. Ladle the soup into bowls, and top each with a Cheddar crouton. Serve with additional croutons on the side for dipping.

Thai Roasted Carrot-Ginger Soup

Prep time: 20 minutes • Cook time: 1 hour, 15 minutes

GLUTEN-FREE, NUT-FREE, VEGAN OPTION

It's hard to believe this ultra-silky soup contains no dairy! It's creamy and elegant, with a spicy edge that makes it exciting. I adapted the base for the soup from my go-to recipe for Thai red curry, which is made with ginger, garlic, onions, red curry paste, coconut milk, brown sugar, and a touch of fish sauce for a salty-sweet tang. You can find red curry paste and Asian fish sauce in the Asian food aisle of most grocery stores or online. SERVES 4

8 medium carrots (about 1 pound), trimmed, peeled, and cut into 1-inch pieces

1 tablespoon grapeseed or canola oil

Salt

Freshly ground black pepper

1 large garlic clove, peeled

1 tablespoon peeled and coarsely chopped fresh ginger

½ medium onion, coarsely chopped

1 tablespoon extra-virgin coconut oil (or grapeseed or canola oil)

1½ teaspoons red curry paste

1 (13½-ounce) can coconut milk

4 cups water, divided

½ teaspoon Asian fish sauce (omit if vegan)

½ teaspoon brown sugar

1 tablespoon freshly squeezed lime juice

Lime wedges, for serving

1. Preheat the oven to 375°F. Line a baking sheet with foil. Add the carrots, and drizzle with the grapeseed oil. Season with salt and pepper, and toss to coat. Roast the carrots until they are tender and browned, stirring occasionally, about 45 to 60 minutes.

2. In the meantime, fit the food processor with the *s blade*. With the motor running, drop the garlic through the feed tube to chop. Add the ginger and onion, and pulse until finely chopped, about 10 pulses.

3. In a medium saucepan over medium heat, melt the coconut oil. Scrape the garlic mixture from the food processor into the pan, and season with salt and pepper. Cook, stirring often, until tender and fragrant, about 4 minutes.

4. Add the red curry paste and cook, stirring, for 30 seconds. Add the coconut milk, 2 cups of water, and the fish sauce and brown sugar. Remove the pot from the heat and set aside until the carrots are ready.

5. When the carrots are roasted, scrape them into the saucepan. Bring to a boil then reduce to a simmer and cook for 10 minutes, or until the carrots are very tender. Let cool slightly.

6. Rinse out the food processor and reassemble it with the *s blade*. Carefully transfer the soup to the food processor (you can do this in batches, if needed). Place a towel over the top to avoid splatters, and process until smooth, stopping and scraping down the sides occasionally. Transfer it back to the pot.

7. Add the remaining 2 cups of water and the lime juice, and season with salt and pepper. Reheat over medium low before serving the soup with the lime wedges.

STORAGE The soup can refrigerated for up to 5 days or frozen for up to 2 months. If needed, thin with a splash of water before serving.

TIME SAVER The depth of flavor in this soup comes from roasting the carrots before adding them. This caramelizes their sugars, making them sweet and complex. You can roast the carrots the day before and store them in the refrigerator if you want to get a jump-start. The rest of the soup comes together quickly.

8

Salads

Beet and Apple Slaw

Prep time: 10 minutes

GLUTEN-FREE, VEGAN

Raw beets are sweet, crunchy, and earthy, and here they're partnered with tart green apples, nutty walnuts, and snipped chives for a slaw that's fantastic alongside grilled sausages, chicken, or fish. We even like to pile it right on top of pork, turkey, or veggie burgers. This is a great way to introduce beets to young children (or wary adults). The slaw is not only sweet and mild, but also bright fuchsia, which helps with the sales pitch—particularly if you have kids who are as princess-obsessed as mine. SERVES 6

2 tablespoons freshly squeezed lemon juice

1 garlic clove, grated on a microplane

1 teaspoon Dijon mustard

Pinch red pepper flakes

Salt

Freshly ground black pepper

3 tablespoons extra-virgin olive oil

2 medium green apples (such as Granny Smith), cored and quartered

4 medium beets (about 1 pound), peeled and quartered

½ cup toasted, chopped walnuts (see How-to, page 37)

2 tablespoons chopped chives

1. In a small bowl, whisk together the lemon juice, garlic, mustard, red pepper flakes, and a pinch of salt and pepper. Whisk in the olive oil.

2. Fit the food processor with the *shredding disc*. Push the apples through the feed tube to shred, followed by the beets.

3. Transfer the vegetables to a large bowl. Add the dressing and toss to coat. Season with salt and pepper. Fold in the walnuts and chives, and serve.

STORAGE The slaw can be refrigerated for up to 2 hours before serving.

Classic Coleslaw

There are as many versions of a "classic" coleslaw as there are grandmothers in the Midwest. While they all consist of shredded cabbage and usually carrots with a mayonnaise-based dressing, the other ingredients vary according to culture and tradition. Hard-boiled eggs, celery, sweet relish, and/or dill pickles are just some of the classic additions. I like to keep it simple. This version, bound with just enough mayonnaise to hug everything together without weighing things down, is seasoned with a touch of apple cider vinegar, honey, and celery seeds, which add a pop of flavor. Feel free to add to it according to your preference (and grandmother). SERVES 6

½ medium head green cabbage, cored

2 medium carrots, trimmed and washed

½ cup mayonnaise

1½ tablespoons raw apple cider vinegar

1½ teaspoons honey

¼ teaspoon celery seeds

Salt

Freshly ground black pepper

SIMPLE SWAP To make a vegan version of this coleslaw, simply swap out the mayo for a vegan mayonnaise, such as Vegenaise, and use maple syrup or sugar in place of the honey.

1. Fit the food processor with the *shredding disc*. Push the cabbage through the feed tube to shred, followed by the carrots.

2. In a large bowl, whisk together the mayonnaise, vinegar, honey, and celery seeds. Season with salt and pepper.

3. Scrape the cabbage and carrots into the bowl with the dressing. Season with salt and pepper, toss to coat, and serve.

STORAGE The slaw can be refrigerated for up to 2 hours before serving.

Red Cabbage and Lime Coleslaw

Prep time: 15 minutes

GLUTEN-FREE, NUT-FREE, VEGETARIAN

We eat a lot of tacos. Whether they're stuffed with chicken, pork, fish, or black beans, I almost always whip up this slaw to serve alongside. With the subtle smokiness of cumin, the gentle heat of jalapeño, and a burst of fresh lime juice, it's bright, crunchy, and vibrant. We also pile it on sandwiches of all stripes (think turkey and avocado, pulled pork, seared tofu, beef, and fish burgers), and it's a great side dish to grilled meats. SERVES 6

½ medium head red cabbage, cored

2 medium carrots, trimmed and washed

2 tablespoons freshly squeezed lime juice

1 garlic clove, grated on a microplane

1 teaspoon ground cumin

½ cup mayonnaise

Salt

Freshly ground black pepper

1 cup lightly packed chopped fresh cilantro (from about 1 bunch)

⅓ cup finely chopped red onion (from about ¼ medium onion), rinsed in cold water

1 jalapeño pepper, seeded and finely chopped

INGREDIENT INFO While I love the flavor of raw onions, I don't love how that flavor can linger for the rest of the day. The red onions are rinsed to get rid of their bite before being added to the salad, meaning you won't be tasting them at your next meal.

1. Fit the food processor with the *shredding disc*. Push the cabbage through the feed tube to shred, followed by the carrots.

2. In a large bowl, whisk together the lime juice, garlic, cumin, and mayonnaise. Season with salt and pepper.

3. Scrape the cabbage and carrots into the bowl with the dressing. Add the cilantro, red onion, and jalapeño. Season with salt and pepper, toss to coat, and serve.

STORAGE The slaw can be refrigerated for up to 2 hours before serving.

Shaved Brussels Sprouts Salad with Walnuts and Parmigiano

Prep time: 15 minutes

GLUTEN-FREE, VEGETARIAN

The first time I ate raw Brussels sprouts was close to a decade ago, when my husband and I lived in Brooklyn. The sprouts were thinly shaved and served in a simple but absolutely delicious salad with walnuts and Parmesan. It was a revelation! Luckily, the food processor makes the prep a breeze, shaving the sprouts in the time it would take to slice a few by hand. For the best flavor, use sprouts with tight heads and bright green leaves, good-quality cold-pressed extra-virgin olive oil, and Italian Parmigiano-Reggiano. SERVES 4 TO 6

1 ½ pounds Brussels sprouts

½ cup toasted walnuts, coarsely chopped (see How-to, page 37)

2 to 3 ounces shaved Parmigiano-Reggiano cheese

Kosher salt

Freshly ground black pepper

3 tablespoons freshly squeezed lemon juice

6 to 7 tablespoons good-quality extra-virgin olive oil

1. Remove and discard the tough outer leaves of the Brussels sprouts, and trim off the ends.

2. Fit the food processor with the *shredding disc*. Push the Brussels sprouts through the feed tube to shred.

3. Transfer the sprouts to a large bowl, and add the walnuts and shaved Parmigiano. Season with salt and pepper.

4. In a small bowl, whisk the lemon juice with 6 tablespoons of olive oil. Season with salt and pepper. Pour the dressing over the salad, and toss to coat. Taste, season with additional salt, pepper, or olive oil as needed, and serve.

Quinoa Tabbouleh Salad

Prep time: 20 minutes, plus 30 minutes to chill

GLUTEN-FREE, NUT-FREE, VEGAN

Tabbouleh is made with a ton of chopped parsley, mint, scallions, and garlic, which take ages to finely chop by hand. While tabbouleh is traditionally made with bulgur wheat, I've swapped in quinoa, which lends delicious texture and flavor—and happens to be gluten-free. This is the perfect side dish to the Falafel (page 208). To make this into a main dish, add chickpeas and feta. SERVES 4 TO 6

2 garlic cloves, peeled

1 bunch fresh flat leaf parsley, leaves and upper stems only

¼ cup packed fresh mint leaves

2 scallions, coarsely chopped

2 cups cooked quinoa (see How-to)

1 cup finely diced seedless (English) cucumber

1 cup finely diced seeded tomatoes or halved grape tomatoes

¼ teaspoon ground cumin

2 tablespoons freshly squeezed lemon juice

3 tablespoons extra-virgin olive oil

Kosher salt

Freshly ground black pepper

HOW-TO To cook 1 cup of quinoa, rinse it well in cold water then put it in a medium pot. Cover by 1 inch with cold water, and add a pinch of salt. Bring to a boil then reduce to a simmer and cook, covered, for 10 minutes, or until the quinoa is tender and just starts to unfurl. Drain. 1 cup of uncooked quinoa will yield about 3 cups of cooked quinoa.

1. Fit the food processor with the *s blade*. With the motor running, drop the garlic cloves through the feed tube to chop. Stop and scrape down the sides.

2. Add the parsley, mint, and scallions. Process until finely chopped.

3. Transfer the herbs to a large bowl, and add the quinoa, cucumber, tomatoes, cumin, lemon juice, and olive oil. Season with salt and pepper. Cover and refrigerate for 30 minutes to allow the flavors to meld.

4. Before serving, taste again and season with additional salt, pepper, or olive oil as needed.

STORAGE The tabbouleh can be refrigerated for up to 8 hours before serving.

Shredded Carrot Salad with Chile, Mint, and Sesame Seeds

Prep time: 15 minutes

GLUTEN-FREE, NUT-FREE, VEGAN

I ate my first shredded carrot salad when I was studying abroad in France as a college student. The carrots were tossed with a Dijon vinaigrette, and I was struck at how simple yet flavorful it was. I've since made about a million different shredded carrot salads, but this is my favorite. It's sweet, a tad spicy, and loaded with flavor—perfect alongside grilled or braised meats, fish, or grains. SERVES 4 TO 6

3 tablespoons freshly squeezed lime juice

1 garlic clove, grated on a microplane

½ jalapeño pepper, seeded and inner ribs discarded, finely chopped

½ teaspoon ground cumin

2 teaspoons toasted sesame oil

1 teaspoon maple syrup

Salt

Freshly ground black pepper

6 tablespoons extra-virgin olive oil

8 medium carrots (about 1 pound), trimmed

2 scallions, thinly sliced

¼ cup lightly packed fresh mint leaves, coarsely chopped

¼ cup toasted sesame seeds

1. In a small bowl, whisk together the lime juice, garlic, jalapeño, cumin, sesame oil, and maple syrup. Season with salt and pepper. Whisk in the olive oil.

2. Fit the food processor with the *shredding disc*. Push the carrots through the feed tube to shred. Transfer to a bowl, and add the dressing. Toss to coat.

3. Fold in the scallions, mint, and sesame seeds. Season with salt and pepper, and serve.

STORAGE The salad can be refrigerated for up to 1 day.

INGREDIENT INFO You'll notice that I don't call for peeling the carrots in this recipe (or in several others throughout the book). That's because carrot peel is loaded with nutrients. Plus, it saves a step— I'm all about anything that saves time *and* is good for you! If you're not peeling, however, it's important to scrub them well and to use organic carrots, as pesticide residues are harbored in the peel.

Napa Cabbage Salad with Peanut Dressing

Prep time: 20 minutes

GLUTEN-FREE OPTION, VEGETARIAN

I could eat this creamy peanut dressing with a spoon, but that would mean there wouldn't be enough left for the salad. This is everything I want a salad to be: crunchy, refreshing, and loaded with flavor. Even my peanut butter-hating child (seriously, what kid hates peanut butter?) will eat this, as long as I keep the chopped peanuts and peppers off her portion (it's always a compromise). Serve the salad as a side dish to grilled meats such as the Asian Marinated Pork Chops (page 188), or make it a main course by tossing in some shredded chicken. SERVES 4 TO 6

¼ cup roasted peanuts

1 large garlic clove, peeled

1 teaspoon peeled and coarsely chopped fresh ginger

2 tablespoons peanut butter

2 teaspoons gluten-free tamari or soy sauce

2 teaspoons toasted sesame oil

2 tablespoons rice vinegar

⅛ teaspoon red pepper flakes

2 teaspoons honey

¼ cup grapeseed or canola oil

Salt

Freshly ground black pepper

½ medium head napa cabbage, thinly sliced

½ red bell pepper, very thinly sliced

1½ cups snow peas, trimmed and cut into thirds

2 scallions, thinly sliced

¼ cup coarsely chopped fresh cilantro

STORAGE The dressing can be refrigerated for up to 3 days. Bring to room temperature before serving.

1. Fit the mini food processor with the *s blade*. Add the peanuts, and pulse until finely chopped. Transfer to a small bowl.

2. Reassemble the processor (no need to wash). Add the garlic and ginger. Process until finely chopped. Stop and scrape down the sides.

3. Add the peanut butter, tamari, sesame oil, rice vinegar, red pepper flakes, honey, and grapeseed oil. Season with salt and pepper. Process until smooth. Taste and season with additional salt and pepper as needed.

4. Place the napa cabbage, red pepper, snow peas, scallions, cilantro, and reserved peanuts in a large bowl, and season with salt and pepper. Drizzle the dressing over the salad, toss to coat, and serve.

Chopped Power Salad

Prep time: 15 minutes, plus 10 minutes to sit

GLUTEN-FREE, NUT-FREE, VEGAN

This salad is super nutritious, but it tastes so good that you won't even care how healthy it is. The food processor makes quick work out of finely chopping everything, and the result is a riot of flavor, color, and texture. Even though each vegetable gets chopped separately in the processor, there's no need to wash the bowl between each batch, meaning the process goes quickly. SERVES 6

3 cups cauliflower florets (about 1 small head)

3 cups broccoli florets (about 1 small head)

2 medium carrots, trimmed and coarsely chopped

1 garlic clove, peeled

⅓ cup lightly packed fresh parsley leaves

⅓ cup lightly packed fresh cilantro leaves

⅓ cup golden raisins

⅓ cup toasted pumpkin seeds (see How-to, page 37)

¼ cup raw apple cider vinegar

½ cup extra-virgin olive oil

Salt

Freshly ground black pepper

1. Fit the food processor with the *s blade*. Add the cauliflower, and pulse until finely chopped, about 15 to 20 pulses. Scrape into a large bowl.

2. Reassemble the food processor, and add the broccoli. Pulse until finely chopped, about 15 to 20 pulses. Scrape into the bowl.

3. Reassemble the food processor, and add the carrots. Process until finely chopped, about 10 seconds. Scrape into the bowl.

4. Reassemble the food processor (this is the last time!). With the motor running, drop the garlic through the feed tube to chop. Stop and scrape down the sides. Add the parsley and cilantro. Process until the herbs are finely chopped. Scrape the mixture into the bowl.

5. Stir the raisins, pumpkin seeds, vinegar, and olive oil into the salad, and season with salt and pepper. Toss to coat. Let the salad sit for at least 10 minutes to let the flavors meld, or refrigerate for up to 2 hours. Before serving, add additional salt, pepper, olive oil, or vinegar as needed.

STORAGE The salad can be refrigerated for up to 2 hours before serving.

INGREDIENT INFO Raw apple cider vinegar, which has not been heated or filtered, is rich in enzymes and potassium and is known for its health properties, such as promoting digestion. If you can't find it, use regular cider vinegar or freshly squeezed lemon juice.

Fish & Seafood Dinners

Salmon Burgers with Yogurt Dill Sauce

Prep time: 25 minutes • Cook time: 10 minutes

GLUTEN-FREE OPTION, NUT-FREE

I've discovered that I can slip nearly any meat, vegetable, or grain down my five-year-old, as long as it's in burger form. I suspect it's because she loves any opportunity to eat, totally acceptably, with her hands. But even if you're not so finger-food inclined, you're still going to love these salmon burgers. They can either be served in buns or over a salad (I love them with a cool cucumber salad). If you'd like, top the burgers with an ultrasimple yogurt dill sauce. I prefer to buy fresh salmon, but if it's not available, this recipe works great with frozen wild salmon—just defrost it partially and skip the freezer step. SERVES 4

FOR THE YOGURT DILL SAUCE

½ cup plain yogurt

1 small garlic clove, grated on a microplane

1 tablespoon chopped dill

Kosher salt

Freshly ground black pepper

FOR THE SALMON BURGERS

1 pound skinless salmon fillet

2 scallions, coarsely chopped

1 tablespoon lightly packed fresh parsley leaves

1 tablespoon dill fronds

1 teaspoon freshly squeezed lemon juice

2 teaspoons Dijon mustard

2 tablespoons Panko bread crumbs (regular or gluten-free)

Kosher salt

Freshly ground black pepper

2 tablespoons grapeseed or canola oil

TO MAKE THE YOGURT DILL SAUCE

In a small bowl, combine the yogurt, garlic, and dill. Season with salt and pepper to taste. Cover and refrigerate until ready to use.

TO MAKE THE SALMON BURGERS

1. Cut the salmon into 1-inch pieces, and spread them in an even layer on a plate. Put the plate in the freezer for 10 minutes while you prepare the other ingredients.

2. Fit the food processor with the *s blade.* Add the scallions, parsley, and dill. Process until finely chopped. Stop and scrape down the sides.

3. Add the salmon, lemon juice, Dijon mustard, and Panko bread crumbs and season with salt and pepper. Pulse until the fish is finely chopped, about 20 pulses.

4. Line a plate with wax or parchment paper. Form the salmon mixture into 4 patties, and arrange them on the plate. If you have the time, cover the plate with plastic wrap and refrigerate for 30 minutes or up to 4 hours (this will help the burgers keep their shape). If not, they can be cooked directly.

HOW-TO Why freeze? Putting the salmon in the freezer for 10 minutes firms up the flesh, enabling the processor to evenly chop the salmon without turning it into a paste.

5. In a large nonstick skillet over medium-high heat, heat the grapeseed oil. Add the burgers and cook until browned on the bottom, about 5 minutes. Flip and cook until browned on the other side and cooked to your liking, about 5 minutes.

6. Serve the burgers with a dollop of the yogurt dill sauce, either in buns with your favorite burger fixings, or over a salad.

STORAGE The uncooked salmon burgers can be placed on a wax or parchment paper-lined plate, covered with plastic wrap, and refrigerated for up to 4 hours before cooking.

Coconut-Curry Rice Bowls with Shrimp

Prep time: 20 minutes • Cook time: 15 minutes

GLUTEN-FREE

The food processor is queen when it comes to making curry pastes from scratch. It easily breaks down the aromatics, and the resulting flavors are a thousand times more vivid and bright than curry pastes out of a jar. This is a dish I crave. It's spicy, sweet, salty, and everything delicious. Don't be intimated by the ingredient list here—these items can now be found at most supermarkets, and once everything gets going, the curry comes together quickly. Be sure to serve with spoons to slurp up the sauce! SERVES 4

1 lemongrass stalk, bottom 6 to 7 inches only

1 large garlic clove, peeled

1 jalapeño pepper, halved, seeded, and inner ribs discarded

2 medium shallots, peeled and coarsely chopped

1 tablespoon peeled and coarsely chopped fresh ginger

¼ teaspoon ground turmeric

1 tablespoon Asian fish sauce

2 tablespoons grapeseed or canola oil, divided

1 cup unsweetened canned coconut milk

1½ cups water

2 teaspoons packed light brown sugar

Kosher salt

2 cups snow peas

1 pound medium peeled and deveined shrimp

3 cups cooked jasmine rice, for serving

¼ cup chopped, toasted cashews, for serving (see How-to, page 37)

Lime wedges, for serving

1. Trim off the bottom brown nub of the lemongrass stalk, and peel away the outer 2 or 3 layers, leaving you with a pale white piece. Cut it crosswise into ¼-inch slices.

2. Fit the food processor with the *s blade*. With the motor running, drop the garlic clove through the feed tube, followed by the jalapeño. Process to chop. Add the lemongrass, shallots, and ginger. Process until finely chopped. Stop and scrape down the sides.

3. Add the turmeric, fish sauce, and 1 tablespoon of grapeseed oil. Process to a paste, stopping and scraping down the sides often until you have a fairly smooth purée.

4. In a bowl or a large liquid measuring cup, stir to combine the coconut milk, water, and brown sugar.

5. In a 12-inch heavy-bottomed skillet over medium-low heat, heat the remaining 1 tablespoon of grapeseed oil. Add the spice paste, and cook, stirring, until the mixture darkens slightly and starts to caramelize, 5 to 8 minutes. Adjust the heat to low if the mixture looks like it's cooking too quickly.

6. Carefully add the coconut milk mixture, and season with salt. Bring to a boil then reduce to a simmer and cook, stirring occasionally, for 5 minutes. Add the snow peas and shrimp, and cook just until the shrimp are pink and curled, 5 to 8 minutes. Taste and season with salt as needed.

7. Divide the rice among 4 shallow bowls, and ladle the curry over the rice. Garnish each bowl with the toasted cashews, and serve with the lime wedges.

Seared Scallops with Roasted Red Pepper and Black Olive Relish

Prep time: 20 minutes • Cook time: 10 minutes

GLUTEN-FREE, NUT-FREE

One night I was looking for a way to dress up a few pork chops I had pulled out of the freezer, and pulsed together a quick relish. It ended up being the perfect salty-sweet complement to the chops. Since then I've tucked this relish into sandwiches and spooned it over chicken and fish. I especially love it with seared scallops. The scallops are browned until caramelized and tender, then drizzled with a quick balsamic pan sauce. The relish gets spooned over the top, lending a bright burst of flavor. SERVES 4

FOR THE RELISH

1 small shallot, coarsely chopped
  (about 2 tablespoons)

1 large garlic clove, peeled

2 tablespoons extra-virgin olive oil, divided

1 teaspoon finely chopped fresh thyme

Kosher salt

Freshly ground black pepper

¾ cup coarsely chopped jarred roasted
  red peppers

⅓ cup pitted Kalamata olives

1 tablespoon drained capers

2 tablespoons coarsely chopped fresh parsley

1 teaspoon freshly squeezed lemon juice

1 teaspoon sugar

FOR THE SCALLOPS

1½ pounds large sea scallops
  (about 3 to 5 scallops per person,
  depending on their size)

Kosher salt

Freshly ground black pepper

1 tablespoon butter

1 tablespoon extra-virgin olive oil

¼ cup balsamic vinegar

TO MAKE THE RELISH

1. Fit the mini food processor with the *s blade*. Add the shallot and garlic. Process until finely chopped.

2. In a small skillet over medium-low heat, heat 1 tablespoon of olive oil. Add the shallots and garlic, the thyme, and season with salt and pepper. Cook, stirring occasionally, until the shallots and garlic are softened, about 2 minutes. Scrape the mixture, including the oil, into a small bowl.

3. Reassemble the mini food processor with the *s blade* (no need to wash). Add the roasted red peppers, Kalamata olives, capers, and parsley. Pulse 5 times then stop and scrape down the sides. Pulse another 5 times then stop and scrape again. Pulse again until the red peppers and olives are finely chopped but not puréed, about 4 more pulses.

4. Transfer the olive mixture to the bowl with the garlic and shallots. Stir in the lemon juice, sugar, and the remaining 1 tablespoon of olive oil. Taste and season with salt and pepper as needed. Leave at room temperature for up to 2 hours or refrigerate for up to 5 days.

TO MAKE THE SCALLOPS

1. Pat the scallops dry. If the tough muscle on the side is attached, remove and discard it from each scallop. Season with salt and pepper on both sides.

2. In a large nonstick skillet over medium-high heat, heat the butter and olive oil. When the butter is melted and hot, add the scallops. Cook without moving until dark golden brown on the bottom, 3 to 5 minutes. Flip and cook for 1 to 2 minutes longer, or until just cooked through. Transfer to a plate, seared-side up.

3. Discard any oil in the skillet; place the skillet back over medium-high heat. Add the balsamic vinegar (stand back to avoid spatter!), and bring to a boil, scraping up the brown bits from the bottom of the pan with a wooden spoon. Reduce the balsamic by about half, or until it becomes syrupy with very large bubbles, 1 to 2 minutes. Remove the pan from the heat.

4. To serve, arrange the scallops on plates or on a platter. Drizzle with the balsamic glaze, and spoon a bit of the relish over each. Serve with additional relish at the table.

INGREDIENT INFO When buying scallops, you want to ask for "dry" as opposed to "wet" scallops. Wet-packed scallops have been treated with a chemical solution that plumps them up and increases their shelf life, but they end up leaching out a lot of water when cooking, and it's impossible to get a good sear. Dry scallops are stored without chemicals or preservatives. They will not only sear far better, but they also have a fresher, purer flavor.

STORAGE The relish can be refrigerated for up to 5 days.

Shrimp Tacos with Pumpkin Seed and Spinach Pesto

Prep time: 25 minutes, plus 6 hours to soak • Cook time: 5 minutes

GLUTEN-FREE, NUT-FREE

In these tacos, sautéed shrimp get tossed with a super nutritious pumpkin seed and spinach pesto, which has a bright, nutty flavor. The shrimp are layered into corn tortillas with avocado slices, a lime-dressed napa cabbage slaw, and hot sauce (I'll take an extra drizzle, please). My husband and daughter also like a dollop of sour cream. The pumpkin seeds for the pesto need to soak for 6 to 10 hours, so start them in the morning or the night before. SERVES 4

FOR THE PESTO

¼ cup raw pumpkin seeds (pepitas)

1 garlic clove, peeled

½ jalapeño pepper, seeded, inner ribs discarded

½ cup lightly packed fresh cilantro leaves

1 cup lightly packed baby spinach leaves

Juice of ½ lime, plus more for seasoning

Kosher salt

Freshly ground black pepper

¼ cup extra-virgin olive oil

FOR THE TACOS

2 tablespoons freshly squeezed lime juice

4 tablespoons extra-virgin olive oil, divided

Kosher salt

Freshly ground black pepper

1 pound shelled and deveined wild shrimp, tails discarded

4 cups shredded napa cabbage (about ½ head)

Warm corn tortillas, for serving

Avocado slices, for serving

Hot sauce, for serving

Sour cream, for serving (optional)

TO MAKE THE PESTO

1. In a medium bowl, cover the pumpkin seeds with warm water and soak for 6 to 10 hours. Drain and rinse.

2. Fit the food processor with the *s blade*. With the motor running, drop the garlic and jalapeño through the feed tube to chop. Stop and scrape down the sides.

3. Add the drained pumpkin seeds and the cilantro, spinach, and lime juice, and season with salt and pepper. Process until finely chopped, stopping and scraping down the sides as needed.

4. With the motor running, slowly drizzle in the olive oil. Taste and season with additional salt, pepper, and lime juice, if desired.

TO MAKE THE TACOS

1. In a small bowl, make a dressing by whisking together the lime juice and 3 tablespoons of olive oil. Season with salt and pepper, and set aside.

2. Season the shrimp with salt and pepper. In a large nonstick or cast iron skillet over medium-high heat, heat the remaining 1 tablespoon of olive oil. Add the shrimp, and arrange in a single layer. Cook until pink on the bottom, about 1½ to 2 minutes. Turn and cook until cooked through—they should be white throughout—about 1½ to 2 minutes more. Transfer to a large bowl, and add ⅓ cup of the pumpkin seed and spinach pesto. Toss well to coat.

3. In a large bowl, toss the cabbage with the lime dressing. Season with salt and pepper.

4. To assemble the tacos, pile a few shrimp on a warm tortilla and top with avocado slices, some of the dressed napa cabbage, a drizzle of hot sauce, and a dollop of sour cream, if desired. Serve immediately.

INGREDIENT INFO In this recipe, you want to use hulled, green pumpkin seeds, often referred to as pepitas, not the white ones you dig out of your Halloween pumpkins. Pumpkin seeds are nutrient-rich, containing fiber, zinc, potassium, protein, and iron.

STORAGE The pumpkin seed pesto can be refrigerated for up to 5 days.

Crispy Maple-Walnut–Crusted Salmon

Prep time: 15 minutes • Cook time: 15 minutes

GLUTEN-FREE OPTION

You know those nights when you find out that friends are unexpectedly coming over (or were unknowingly invited by your spouse) and you have exactly four minutes to race into the grocery store and figure out what to make for dinner? This is what you make. You probably even already have most of the ingredients at home. It's insanely simple but impressively elegant. SERVES 4

1 tablespoon Dijon mustard

1 tablespoon maple syrup

½ teaspoon finely chopped fresh
  rosemary, divided

1 small garlic clove, grated on a microplane

Salt

Freshly ground black pepper

1 slice whole-wheat or white, or gluten-free
  bread, torn into pieces

⅓ cup walnuts

1 tablespoon extra-virgin olive oil,
  plus more for brushing

4 (6-ounce) salmon fillets

1. Preheat the oven to 400°F, and place a rack in the middle.

2. In a small bowl, mix together the mustard, maple syrup, ¼ teaspoon of rosemary, and the garlic. Season with salt and pepper.

3. Fit the mini food processor with the *s blade*. Add the bread, and process to coarse crumbs. Transfer to a medium bowl.

4. Place the walnuts in the processor (no need to clean), and process until finely chopped. Add the walnuts to the bread crumbs, along with the remaining ¼ teaspoon of rosemary. Season with salt and pepper. Pour in the olive oil, and toss to coat.

5. Line a baking sheet with foil, and brush it with olive oil. Place the salmon fillets on the baking sheet, and season with salt and pepper. Brush the Dijon mixture over the tops and sides of each, then top with the bread crumb and nut mixture, pressing to form a crust.

6. Roast for 8 to 12 minutes, or until the salmon flakes easily but is still very pink in the middle, or until cooked through, and serve.

Grilled Halibut with Smoky Red Pepper Sauce

Prep time: 10 minutes · Cook time: 10 minutes
GLUTEN-FREE

I tossed together this smoky red pepper sauce one night to dress up a simple bowl of roasted vegetables. The sauce—which is actually a cross between a sauce, a pesto, and a dressing—moved the vegetables to center stage. I've since slathered it on fried eggs, roasted chicken, skirt steak, and fish, and I think it tastes especially brilliant with grilled halibut. It's super simple but has a tantalizing flavor and vivid color, like a sexy little red dress for the fish. SERVES 4

1 garlic clove, peeled

1 cup coarsely chopped jarred roasted red peppers

3 tablespoons toasted pine nuts (see How-to, page 37)

⅛ teaspoon ground smoked paprika

⅛ teaspoon sugar

Kosher salt

Freshly ground black pepper

2 tablespoons extra-virgin olive oil, plus more for brushing

4 (6-ounce) halibut steaks or fillets

½ tablespoon finely chopped fresh rosemary

STORAGE The smoky red pepper sauce can be refrigerated for up to 5 days.

1. Fit the mini food processor with the *s blade*. Add the garlic clove, and process to chop. Add the roasted red peppers, pine nuts, smoked paprika, and sugar. Season with salt and pepper. Process until smooth, stopping and scraping down the sides as needed.

2. With the motor running, slowly pour the olive oil through the feed tube or through one of the holes in the lid. Taste and season with additional salt, pepper, and sugar as needed.

3. Preheat a grill or grill pan to medium high. Clean and oil the grill grates. Brush the halibut with olive oil and sprinkle with the rosemary. Season on both sides with salt and pepper.

4. Grill the fish for 3 to 4 minutes per side, or until opaque throughout. Transfer to a platter or plates, and spoon the smoky red pepper sauce over the top. Serve with additional sauce at the table.

Seared Snapper with Green Gazpacho Sauce

Prep time: 15 minutes • Cook time: 10 minutes

GLUTEN-FREE, NUT-FREE

I used to run a cooking school at Rainbeau Ridge Farm in Bedford Hills, New York, where I would teach classes as well as host guest chefs. One season I hosted the chef from Mount Kisco Seafood, John Everin, who made a version of this dish. It wowed me with its simplicity and elegance. Cumin-dusted seared snapper is served over a cooling cucumber gazpacho sauce that is made in minutes in the food processor. The warm fish with the cool sauce is unforgettable. Since the whole meal comes together in about 20 minutes, this is the ideal summer dinner, preferably eaten outside with a cold glass of white wine. SERVES 4

1½ cups coarsely chopped seedless (English) cucumber

¼ cup coarsely chopped scallions

¼ cup lightly packed fresh cilantro leaves

1 jalapeño pepper, seeded and coarsely chopped

1 tablespoon white balsamic vinegar

Kosher salt

Freshly ground black pepper

4 tablespoons extra-virgin olive oil, divided

4 (6-ounce) skin-on red snapper fillets

1 teaspoon ground cumin

1 cup cherry tomatoes, halved

Flaky sea salt, for serving (optional)

Good-quality extra-virgin olive oil, for serving

1. Fit the food processor with the *s blade*. Add the cucumbers, scallions, cilantro, jalapeño, and vinegar, and season generously with salt and pepper. Process until smooth, stopping and scraping down the sides occasionally.

2. With the motor running, slowly drizzle in 2 tablespoons of olive oil. Taste and season with additional salt and pepper as needed. Pour the sauce into 4 shallow bowls.

3. Season the snapper with salt and pepper on both sides. Sprinkle the cumin evenly over the flesh side of each fillet.

4. In a large nonstick skillet over medium-high heat, heat the remaining 2 tablespoons of olive oil. Carefully add the fish fillets, skin-side down. Cook, pressing down on each fillet with a spatula to flatten (this will help crisp up the skin). Cook until the skin is golden brown, 3 to 4 minutes. Flip the fish over, and cook for another 1 to 3 minutes, until just opaque in the center.

5. Place each fish fillet, skin-side up, in the sauce. Garnish each plate with the cherry tomatoes. Sprinkle with flaky sea salt if you wish, and drizzle with good-quality extra-virgin olive oil. Serve immediately.

SIMPLE SWAP Skinless fillets of sea bass or halibut are also delicious in this recipe. You can also grill the fish, if you prefer.

Roasted White Fish
with Chermoula

Prep time: 15 minutes, plus 15 minutes to marinate • Cook time: 15 minutes

GLUTEN-FREE, NUT-FREE

Chermoula is a Moroccan condiment made with cilantro, parsley, garlic, cumin, coriander, and lemon that's usually used as a marinade for seafood. It's bright and lively, with a unique flavor that comes from the freshly toasted whole spices. Here the sauce coats fillets of halibut or sea bass before roasting, turning a simple dinner into something spectacular, with minimal effort. The fish can also be grilled. SERVES 4

2 teaspoons cumin seeds

½ teaspoon coriander seeds

2 garlic cloves, peeled

1½ cups lightly packed fresh cilantro leaves

1 cup lightly packed fresh parsley leaves

2 tablespoons freshly squeezed lemon juice

Kosher salt

Freshly ground black pepper

½ cup extra-virgin olive oil, plus more for brushing

4 (6-ounce) fillets of skinless firm white fish such as halibut or striped bass

1. In a small skillet over medium heat, cook the cumin and coriander seeds, stirring often, until the seeds are lightly toasted and fragrant, 2 to 3 minutes. Cool completely. Grind the spices in a mortar and pestle or a spice grinder.

2. Fit the food processor with the *s blade*. With the motor running, drop the garlic cloves through the feed tube, and process until finely chopped. Add the cilantro, parsley, lemon juice, and ground spices, and season with salt and pepper. Process to a coarse paste, stopping and scraping down the sides occasionally.

3. With the motor running, drizzle the olive oil through the feed tube to incorporate. Taste and season with additional salt and pepper as needed. Place ¼ cup of the chermoula in a bowl, and set aside.

4. Brush a small baking dish (big enough to fit the fish in one layer) with olive oil. Arrange the fish in the dish, and season with salt and pepper. Pour the remaining chermoula over the fish, lifting the fillets to coat all sides. Cover and refrigerate for 15 to 20 minutes.

5. Preheat the oven to 450°F.

6. Roast the fish for 10 to 15 minutes, or until opaque throughout and lightly browned on top. Serve with the reserved chermoula.

STORAGE The chermoula can be refrigerated for up to 2 days. Bring to room temperature before serving.

Poultry & Meat Dinners

Sriracha Chicken Wings

Prep time: 20 minutes, plus 8 hours to marinate • Cook time: 35 minutes

GLUTEN-FREE OPTION, NUT-FREE

My husband loves chicken wings. While he's always preferred the classic Buffalo style, he now begs for these. They're sweet, salty, sticky, and all things awesome. Best of all, since they're baked instead of fried, I don't mind making them often—particularly since I'm the only person who loves wings more than he does. I use the mini processor to buzz up a ginger, honey, and sriracha marinade—and the longer they marinate, the better. Make sure to serve these with extra napkins for sticky fingers! SERVES 4

3 pounds chicken wings or wingettes

4 garlic cloves, peeled

2 tablespoons peeled and coarsely chopped fresh ginger

¼ cup gluten-free tamari or soy sauce

2 tablespoons rice vinegar

2 teaspoons toasted sesame oil

5 tablespoons honey, divided

4 tablespoons sriracha, divided

2 tablespoons grapeseed or canola oil, plus more for brushing

Kosher salt

Freshly ground black pepper

3 tablespoons butter

1. If using whole chicken wings, cut off and discard the wing tips using kitchen shears. Cut the wings in half at the joint. Put the chicken wings in a large zip-top bag.

2. Fit the mini food processor with the *s blade*. Add the garlic cloves and ginger. Process to finely chop. Scrape the sides.

3. Add the tamari, rice vinegar, the sesame oil, 2 tablespoons of honey, 2 tablespoons of the sriracha, and the oil. Process until smooth. Pour the marinade over the chicken wings, seal the bag, and shake to coat evenly. Refrigerate for at least 8 hours or overnight.

4. Preheat the oven to 425°F. Line 2 large baking sheets with foil, and brush them generously with olive oil.

5. Drain the chicken wings, then transfer them to one of the baking sheets. Season with salt and pepper. Arrange in a single layer. Roast for 20 minutes.

6. Turn the wings over, and transfer them to the clean baking sheet. Roast until browned in spots and cooked through, 10 to 15 minutes longer. Transfer the wings to a large bowl.

7. In a small bowl, stir to combine the remaining 3 tablespoons of honey, 2 tablespoons of sriracha, and the butter. Microwave for 60 seconds, or until the butter is melted, or heat in a small pan on the stove.

8. Drizzle the glaze over the wings, and toss to coat. Season well with salt and pepper, if needed. Serve immediately.

Pan-Roasted Chicken Breasts with Romesco Sauce

Prep time: 30 minutes • Cook time: 30 minutes

GLUTEN-FREE

While I like chicken breasts, I find that they're usually fairly bland and often dry. This dish makes me take that all back. These chicken breasts are incredibly juicy and tender, cooked with their skin on to prevent them from drying out and served with a slightly spicy romesco sauce, which hails from the Catalan region of Spain. There are a zillion variations of romesco sauce, but I make mine with dried ancho chiles, roasted red bell peppers, and toasted almonds. For a slightly different flavor, try substituting toasted hazelnuts. SERVES 4

FOR THE SAUCE

4 tablespoons extra-virgin olive oil, divided, plus more for brushing

1 large red bell pepper, halved, seeded, and inner ribs discarded

1 large dried ancho chile

1 plum tomato, seeded and coarsely chopped

2 garlic cloves, thinly sliced

¼ cup toasted almonds (see How-to, page 37)

Pinch red pepper flakes

Pinch sugar

½ teaspoon red wine vinegar

2 tablespoons water

Kosher salt

Freshly ground black pepper

FOR THE CHICKEN

4 boneless, skin-on chicken breasts

3 tablespoons extra-virgin olive oil, divided

Kosher salt

Freshly ground black pepper

6 fresh thyme sprigs

2 fresh rosemary sprigs

6 garlic cloves, unpeeled

½ lemon, cut into 4 wedges

TO MAKE THE SAUCE

1. Preheat the broiler to high, and place a rack 5 to 6 inches from the heating element. Line a small baking sheet with foil, and brush it lightly with olive oil.

2. Fit the food processor with the s *blade*.

3. Place the bell pepper, cut-side down, on the baking sheet. Broil until blackened, about 10 minutes. Cover with foil, and let steam for 10 minutes. Remove and discard the skin and stem. Coarsely chop. (Alternatively, the pepper can be blackened directly on the flame of a gas stove; turn it often for even cooking.) Put the pepper in the food processor.

4. Cut or tear the ancho chile in half, and remove and discard the stem and seeds. In a small skillet over medium heat, heat 2 tablespoons of olive oil. Add the chile, and cook until lightly toasted, 1 to 2 minutes. Transfer the chile to a plate to cool, reserving the oil in the pan. Tear the chile into pieces, and add it to the food processor with the bell pepper.

5. Place the skillet back over medium heat, and add the tomato and garlic. Cook, stirring, until the garlic is fragrant and light golden, about 1 minute. Scrape the tomato, garlic, and oil from the skillet into the food processor.

6. Add the toasted almonds, red pepper flakes, sugar, vinegar, and water to the processor, and season with salt and pepper. Process until lightened in color and nearly smooth, stopping and scraping down the sides occasionally. With the motor running, pour in the remaining 2 tablespoons of olive oil. Process until creamy. Taste and season with additional salt and pepper as needed.

STORAGE The romesco sauce can be refrigerated for up to 5 days.

TO MAKE THE CHICKEN

1. Preheat the oven to 400°F.

2. Drizzle the chicken breasts with 2 tablespoons of olive oil, and rub to coat. Season generously with salt and pepper.

3. In a large ovenproof skillet over medium-high heat, heat the remaining 1 tablespoon of olive oil. Add the chicken, skin-side down, and scatter the thyme, rosemary, garlic cloves, and lemon wedges around the pan. Cook, without moving the chicken, until the skin is golden brown and no longer sticks to the pan, about 9 minutes.

4. Flip the chicken over, and nestle the garlic and herbs alongside. Transfer the skillet to the oven. Cook for 5 to 10 minutes, or until the chicken is just cooked through and the juices run clear.

5. Transfer the chicken to a platter or plates, and serve with the roasted lemon wedges and garlic cloves and the romesco sauce.

INGREDIENT INFO Leaving the skin on the chicken breasts not only imparts incredible flavor, but it also prevents the meat from drying out. If you can't find boneless, skin-on breasts, buy bone-in chicken breasts and ask your butcher to remove the bones for you. Or better yet, cut out the bones yourself and save them for making stock.

Chipotle-Garlic Grilled Chicken

Prep time: 5 minutes, plus 4 hours to marinate, and 15 minutes to sit
Cook time: 35 minutes

GLUTEN-FREE, NUT-FREE

A couple of years ago my mom told me about a chicken marinade she created using canned chipotle peppers and a mess of chopped garlic. I borrowed the idea and fell in love. The preparation is dead simple: Scrape a can of chipotle peppers into a food processor, blitz it with garlic, then slather it on chicken. The marinade gives the chicken a wonderfully spicy, caramelized crust. This chicken is especially delicious with Roasted Smashed Potatoes with Avocado Crema (page 110) and Shredded Carrot Salad with Chile, Mint, and Sesame Seeds (page 146). SERVES 4

5 garlic cloves, peeled
1 (7-ounce) can chipotle peppers in adobo sauce
Kosher salt
Freshly ground black pepper
1 (4-pound) chicken, cut into 8 pieces (2 thighs, 2 legs, 2 breasts, 2 wings), or 4 pounds of your favorite bone-in chicken pieces
Vegetable oil, for oiling

1. Fit the mini food processor with the s blade. Add the garlic, and process to chop. Add the chipotle peppers with their sauce, and season with salt and pepper. Process until mostly smooth, stopping and scraping down the sides occasionally.

2. Place the chicken pieces in a large zip-top bag. Add the chipotle marinade, seal the bag, and shake to coat the chicken. Refrigerate for at least 4 hours or overnight.

3. Remove the chicken pieces from the marinade, and blot off most, but not all, of it. Season with salt and pepper. Let sit at room temperature for 15 minutes to an hour.

4. Prepare a grill with a 2-zone fire, with one side on medium high and one side on medium low. Clean and oil the grill grates. Arrange the chicken, skin-side up, on the medium-low side of the grill. Cover and cook for 25 to 35 minutes, or until cooked through (the internal temperature should read 165°F). Turn the chicken and cook an additional 3 to 6 minutes, until the skin is nicely browned.

5. Alternatively, roast the chicken in a 425°F oven for about 35 minutes, or until cooked through.

6. Transfer to a platter, and let it rest for 5 to 10 minutes before serving.

HOW-TO When grilling chicken, it's all too easy to end up with a charred exterior and an undercooked interior, or worse yet, dried-out meat. To prevent this, I cook bone-in chicken pieces over medium-low heat, starting skin-side up. This allows the chicken to slowly cook, basting itself as the skin renders. When the chicken is cooked through, it's flipped for a few minutes, just to caramelize the skin. You're left with juicy, perfectly cooked chicken.

Chicken and Peach Kebabs with Peanut Dipping Sauce

Prep time: 20 minutes, plus 2 hours to marinate • Cook time: 10 minutes

GLUTEN-FREE OPTION

Don't be intimidated by the list of ingredients here. The peanut sauce—which doubles as a marinade—takes only a few minutes to pull together in the food processor. If peaches or nectarines aren't in season, try chunks of zucchini or red bell pepper instead. The chicken needs to marinate for at least 2 hours, but it's even better if it marinates overnight, making this a perfect prep-ahead dish for a party. You'll need 16 to 20 bamboo skewers for this recipe. SERVES 4

¼ cup roasted peanuts

2 garlic cloves, peeled

1 teaspoon peeled and coarsely chopped fresh ginger

½ cup peanut butter

1 (13½-ounce) can coconut milk

2 tablespoons freshly squeezed lime juice

1 teaspoon low-sodium, gluten-free tamari or soy sauce

1 teaspoon Asian fish sauce

1 tablespoon packed light brown sugar

1 teaspoon sriracha, plus more for serving

Kosher salt

1½ pounds boneless, skinless chicken thighs or breasts, trimmed and cut into 1½-inch chunks

4 or 5 firm but ripe peaches or nectarines, cut into 1½-inch wedges

2 tablespoons finely chopped fresh cilantro

1. Fit the food processor with the *s blade*. Add the peanuts, and pulse until finely chopped, about 8 to 10 pulses. Transfer to a small bowl, and set aside.

2. Reassemble the food processor (no need to wash), and add the garlic cloves and ginger. Process to finely chop. Add the peanut butter, coconut milk, lime juice, tamari, fish sauce, brown sugar, and sriracha, and season with salt. Process until smooth. Taste and season with additional salt as needed. Transfer 1 cup of the peanut sauce to a small bowl, and refrigerate.

3. Put the chicken pieces in a large, zip-top bag, and pour the remaining peanut sauce over the top. Seal the bag and shake to coat the chicken. Refrigerate for at least 2 hours or overnight.

4. Soak the bamboo skewers in water for 1 to 2 hours before cooking.

5. Preheat a grill or stove top grill pan to medium high. Clean and oil the grill grates.

6. Holding 2 skewers parallel to each other about half an inch apart, thread a piece of chicken through both skewers. Thread a wedge of peach through both skewers. Add 2 more pieces of chicken, followed by 1 more peach wedge. Keep repeating, alternating between the chicken and peaches, leaving a bit of space between each.

7. When all the kebabs are assembled, grill them on one side until the chicken is golden brown in spots, 3 to 5 minutes. Flip the skewers, and grill on the other side until the chicken is browned and cooked through, another 3 to 5 minutes.

8. Transfer the kebabs to a platter. Drizzle with some of the reserved peanut sauce, and sprinkle with the chopped peanuts and cilantro. I like to add a drizzle of sriracha as well. Serve with the remaining peanut sauce on the side.

HOW-TO Why two skewers? If you use just one, the peaches and chicken have a tendency to twirl around on the skewers, making them hard to turn over and cook evenly. By using two skewers, you keep the food anchored firmly in place, making flipping a breeze.

Chicken, Greens, and Goat Cheese Quesadillas

Prep time: 15 minutes • Cook time: 15 minutes

NUT-FREE

Warning: It's hard to eat just one of these quesadillas. Crispy on the outside with a mix of chili-spiced chicken, melted Monterey Jack, creamy goat cheese, and spicy mustard greens on the inside—they perfectly balance flavor and texture. If you haven't tried mustard greens before, this is a great time to give them a go. They're extremely nutritious, and they add a subtle kick to the quesadillas without being overpowering. This is my favorite way to use up leftover roasted or rotisserie chicken. SERVES 4 TO 6

1 cup Fresh or Roasted Tomatillo Salsa (page 70), or jarred tomatillo salsa

2 cups packed coarsely chopped mustard green leaves, divided

4 ounces Monterey Jack cheese

2 cups coarsely chopped or shredded cooked chicken

2 teaspoons chili powder

½ teaspoon ground cumin

6 (8-inch) flour tortillas

4 ounces goat cheese, crumbled

2 to 3 tablespoons extra-virgin olive oil, divided

Sour cream, for serving

Avocado slices, for serving

SIMPLE SWAP To make a vegetarian version of these quesadillas, substitute 2 cups of cooked potatoes or beans for the chicken. For a gluten-free version, use gluten-free or corn tortillas.

1. Preheat the oven to 200°F.

2. Fit the food processor with the *s blade*. Add the Tomatillo Salsa and 1 cup of packed mustard greens. Process, stopping and scraping down the sides occasionally, until the greens are fully incorporated into the salsa. Scrape the salsa mixture into a bowl.

3. Wipe out the bowl, and refit the processor with the *shredding disc*. Add the Monterey Jack cheese, and shred. Transfer to a large bowl, and add the chicken, chili powder, and cumin. Toss to combine.

4. Arrange the tortillas on a work surface. Divide the remaining mustard greens over half of each tortilla. Portion the chicken and cheese mixture and the crumbled goat cheese over each, followed by about 2 heaping tablespoons of the salsa mixture. Fold the tortillas in half, and press gently.

5. In a large nonstick skillet over medium heat, heat 1 tablespoon of olive oil. Add 2 quesadillas, and cook until lightly browned on the bottom, 2 to 3 minutes. Flip and cook until browned on the other side, 2 to 3 minutes longer. Transfer to a baking sheet, and place in the oven to keep warm. Repeat with the remaining quesadillas, adding additional oil as needed.

6. Cut the quesadillas into wedges, and serve with sour cream, avocado slices, and another dollop of the salsa mixture.

Individual Chicken Pot Pies

Prep time: 1 hour • Cook time: 50 minutes

NUT-FREE

What's the best part about a chicken pot pie? The buttery, flaky crust. Classic Pie Dough (page 77) is the ultimate topper for an easy but scrumptious chicken stew made with store-bought rotisserie chicken. Since the stew is thickened with cornstarch instead of flour, the pot pies can easily be made gluten-free by using Cup4Cup gluten-free flour in the crust. Also, the pie dough can be made ahead to save on time. This is hands-down my family's favorite cold weather supper. SERVES: 4

4 tablespoons butter

½ medium onion, finely diced

1 stalk celery, finely diced

3 medium carrots, thinly sliced

Kosher salt

Freshly ground black pepper

2 garlic cloves, minced

1 teaspoon chopped fresh thyme

1 bay leaf

4 cups low-sodium chicken broth, divided

3 tablespoons cornstarch

¼ cup crème fraîche

1 cup frozen peas

3 cups shredded rotisserie chicken

1 recipe Classic Pie Dough (made without sugar)

1 egg, beaten

1. Preheat the oven to 375°F.

2. In a large saucepan, melt the butter over medium-high heat. Add the onion, celery, and carrots. Season with salt and pepper. Cook, stirring occasionally, until the vegetables are tender, about 6 minutes. Add the garlic, thyme, and bay leaf. Cook, stirring until fragrant, about 30 seconds.

3. Pour in 3½ cups of the chicken broth and bring to a simmer. Whisk the remaining ½ cup of broth with the cornstarch. Slowly pour the cornstarch mixture into the simmering broth while whisking. Bring to a boil, then reduce to a simmer and cook, stirring occasionally, until slightly thickened, about 5 to 10 minutes.

4. Whisk in the crème fraîche. Add the peas and chicken and season with salt and pepper. Discard the bay leaf. Divide the mixture between 4 ovenproof bowls or dishes.

5. Divide the pie dough into 4 pieces. Roll each into a ¼-inch thick round. Place the dough circles over the pot pies and press down along the edges to trim off the excess dough. Using a fork, press the edges of the dough to seal. Lightly brush the top of each pot pie with some beaten egg (you won't use all the egg). Cut a slit in the top of each as a vent.

6. Transfer the bowls to a large foil-lined baking sheet and bake 45 to 55 minutes, or until the crust is golden brown and the filling is bubbling. Let cool 10 minutes before serving.

TIP If you don't have individual ovenproof bowls, you can make one large pot pie in a 2-quart baking dish.

Marinated Flank Steak with Chimichurri

Prep time: 5 minutes, plus 4 hours to marinate • Cook time: 10 minutes

GLUTEN-FREE OPTION, NUT-FREE

My brother and his wife are excellent cooks, and with four kids (including three-year-old triplets), one of their main sources of entertainment is cooking up incredible meals after the kids go to bed. We vacationed with them last summer, and one night they grilled up marinated skirt steaks that were slightly sweet, salty, and savory. I've recreated their marinade, and I often use it with flank steak, piled into tacos, draped over salads, or drizzled with Chimichurri Sauce—our personal favorite. SERVES 4 TO 6

2 garlic cloves, peeled

1 jalapeño pepper, halved, seeded, and inner ribs discarded

4 scallions, coarsely chopped

½ cup low-sodium, gluten-free tamari or soy sauce

¼ cup freshly squeezed lime juice

3 tablespoons maple syrup

½ teaspoon ground cumin

½ teaspoon dried oregano

½ cup extra-virgin olive oil, plus more for oiling

1½ to 2 pounds flank steak

Kosher salt

Freshly ground black pepper

Chimichurri Sauce, for serving (page 38)

1. Fit the food processor with the *s blade*. With the motor running, drop the garlic cloves and jalapeño through the feed tube to chop. Add the scallions, and process until chopped. Stop and scrape down the sides, and add the tamari, lime juice, maple syrup, cumin, oregano, and olive oil. Process until smooth.

2. Put the flank steak in a large zip-top bag, and pour the marinade over it. Seal the bag, and shake to coat the steak. Refrigerate for at least 4 hours, or overnight, turning occasionally so the marinade evenly coats the meat. Bring to room temperature before proceeding.

3. Preheat a grill or stove top grill pan to medium high. Clean and oil the grill grates. Remove the steak from the marinade, and pat dry with paper towels. Season with salt and pepper. Place the steak on the grill and cook, covered if you're using an outdoor grill, for 3 to 6 minutes, or until the steak is browned with grill marks on the bottom. Flip and cook for an additional 3 to 6 minutes for medium rare (the internal temperature should read 125°F).

4. Transfer the steak to a cutting board, and let it rest for 5 to 10 minutes. Thinly slice the meat against the grain, and transfer to a platter. Drizzle with the Chimichurri Sauce, and serve with additional Chimichurri Sauce on the side.

Tuscan Grilled Skirt Steak with Salsa Verde

Prep time: 10 minutes, plus 30 minutes to marinate, and 10 minutes to sit
Cook time: 10 minutes

GLUTEN-FREE, NUT-FREE

Before my brothers and I had children, we rented a house in Tuscany with our significant others and my parents. Although the trip was incredible, getting there was a bit of a disaster for my husband and me, involving flight delays, missed connections, and inexplicable traffic jams. When we finally arrived, my brothers and dad poured us wine and served us the remnants of their dinner, which had been prepared by a local chef. The first thing I put in my mouth was the most tender, flavorful piece of steak I had ever tasted. It was redolent of garlic, rosemary, and thyme, and it was served with an incredibly flavorful sauce. Our travel debacles disappeared with the first bite. For me, this is the taste of Italy. SERVES 4

3 large garlic cloves, peeled
1 tablespoon coarsely chopped
  fresh rosemary
1 tablespoon fresh thyme leaves
¼ cup extra-virgin olive oil
1¼ to 1½ pounds skirt steak
Kosher salt
Freshly ground black pepper
Italian Salsa Verde, for serving (page 39)

1. Fit the mini food processor with the *s blade*. Add the garlic cloves, rosemary, and thyme. Process until finely chopped. Stop and scrape down the sides, and add the olive oil. Pulse to combine.

2. Trim the steak of any excess fat and cut it in half horizontally, or into thirds for easier grilling. Put the steak pieces in a large zip-top bag and add the garlic-herb mixture. Seal the bag, shake to evenly coat the steak, and let marinate at room temperature for 30 to 60 minutes, or refrigerate for up to 24 hours. If refrigerated, bring the steak to room temperature before proceeding.

3. Preheat a grill or a stove top grill pan to medium high. Clean and oil the grill grates. Remove the steak from the marinade, scraping off most of the garlic, and pat dry. Season with salt and pepper.

4. Place the steak on the grill and cook, (covered if you're using an outdoor grill), until browned with grill marks on the bottom, about 3 to 4 minutes. Turn over and cook until browned on the other side, about 3 to 4 minutes longer for medium rare.

5. Transfer to a cutting board and tent lightly with foil. Let it rest 10 minutes. Thinly slice the meat against the grain and serve with Italian Salsa Verde.

HOW-TO Go against the grain! When slicing steak, you want to be sure to cut across the grain, or in the opposite direction of the tough muscle fibers. This makes the meat much more tender and less chewy. In a skirt steak, you'll notice that the muscle fibers run from side to side. To cut across the grain, you'll therefore need to slice the meat lengthwise. If the piece is too long for your knife, you can always cut it in half before slicing.

Steakhouse Burgers

Prep time: 15 minutes, plus 20 minutes to chill • Cook time: 5 to 10 minutes

NUT-FREE

Maybe it's the fact that I love eating with my hands, but burgers are at the top of my list of favorite foods. We make them about once a week in the summer, when we spend most nights eating outside. Once I started grinding my own meat, it was a complete game-changer. The texture and flavor of these burgers are incomparable—they're supremely beefy and juicy. I think cooking the burgers in a cast iron skillet yields the best flavor, so if we're grilling outside, I simply put the skillet right on the grill over high heat. SERVES 4

1 pound sirloin, cut into ½-inch pieces

½ pound boneless beef short ribs, trimmed, cut into ½-inch pieces

½ medium yellow onion, peeled and coarsely chopped

Kosher salt

Freshly ground black pepper

2 tablespoons grapeseed or canola oil

4 buns

Toppings of your choice, for serving

1. Line a baking sheet with wax paper. Spread the meat out in a single layer. Put the pan in the freezer for 20 minutes, or until the meat is almost firm.

2. Fit the food processor with the *s blade*. Place half the meat in the food processor, and pulse until coarsely ground, about 30 to 40 pulses. Transfer to a large bowl, and repeat with the remaining meat.

3. Reassemble the food processor (no need to wash), and add the onion. Process until very finely chopped. Add the onion to the ground meat, and season with salt and pepper. Toss gently with a fork to combine. Working with a loose touch, form the meat into 4 patties.

4. In a cast iron or heavy-bottomed skillet over medium-high heat, heat the grapeseed oil. Add the burgers and let cook, undisturbed, for 3 to 5 minutes, or until well browned on the bottom. Flip the burgers, and reduce the heat to medium low. Cover and cook for 3 to 5 minutes, or until browned on the other side with an internal temperature of 125°F for medium rare (for medium or well-done burgers, cook for 1 to 3 minutes longer).

5. Transfer to buns, add the toppings of your choice, and serve.

STORAGE The beef patties can be refrigerated for up to 1 day before cooking. Bring to room temperature before cooking.

INGREDIENT INFO "A loose touch" means it's best to handle the meat gently when forming burgers. If you compress it too much, you'll end up with tough burgers, and nobody wants a hockey puck for dinner.

Marinated Lamb Chops
with Mint Pesto

Prep time: 15 minutes, plus 30 minutes to marinate • Cook time: 10 minutes

GLUTEN-FREE

This is my very favorite way to eat—and cook—lamb. When I was growing up, we were always served lamb with neon green mint jelly from a jar. Honestly, it kind of scared me. While I'm not a fan of the sweet jelly and meat pairing, I am definitely a fan of the mint and lamb pairing. In this ultrasimple preparation, mint and parsley form the basis of a vibrant—if not quite so Technicolor—pesto. Serve with the Minty Mashed Peas (page 107). SERVES 4

1 garlic clove, peeled

1½ cups lightly packed fresh mint leaves

1 cup lightly packed fresh parsley leaves

¼ cup toasted pine nuts (see How-to, page 37)

⅛ teaspoon red pepper flakes

1 tablespoon freshly squeezed lemon juice

Kosher salt

Freshly ground black pepper

2 tablespoons water

8 tablespoons extra-virgin olive oil, divided

8 to 12 lamb rib or loin chops, depending on size

1 to 2 tablespoons grapeseed or canola oil

1. Fit the food processor with the *s blade*. With the motor running, drop the garlic clove through the feed tube to chop. Stop and scrape down the sides.

2. Add the mint, parsley, pine nuts, red pepper flakes, and lemon juice. Season with salt and pepper. Process to a coarse purée. Stop and scrape down the sides.

3. With the motor running, drizzle the water and 6 tablespoons of olive oil through the feed tube to incorporate. Taste and season with additional salt and pepper as needed.

4. Measure out ⅓ cup of the pesto, and transfer it to a large zip-top bag. Transfer the rest of the pesto to a small bowl, and refrigerate until ready to use.

5. To the pesto in the bag, add the remaining 2 tablespoons of olive oil. Place the lamb chops in the bag, seal, and shake to evenly coat the chops. Let sit at room temperature for 30 minutes or refrigerate for up to 4 hours. Bring to room temperature before proceeding.

6. Remove the lamb from the marinade. Blot off most, but not all, of the marinade. Season the lamb with salt and pepper on both sides.

7. In a large skillet over medium-high heat, heat 1 tablespoon of grapeseed oil. Working in batches, add the lamb chops, being sure not to overcrowd the pan. Cook until browned on the bottom, about 3 minutes. Flip and cook to desired doneness, 3 to 4 more minutes for medium rare. Transfer to a platter, tent lightly with foil, and repeat with the remaining chops, adding additional oil as needed.

8. Spoon the reserved mint pesto over the lamb chops, and serve.

Asian Marinated Pork Chops with Cilantro and Mint Chutney

Prep time: 25 minutes, plus 4 hours to marinate, and 15 minutes to sit
Cook time: 15 minutes

GLUTEN-FREE OPTION

Juicy, salty, and sweet, these pork chops are one of our very favorite dinners. I'll make the chutney and the marinade for the chops in the morning, so all we have to do is grill the pork chops at dinner time. The chutney has a hint of sweetness from coconut and a hint of spice from jalapeño. I like to serve this with rice and the Napa Cabbage Salad with Peanut Dressing (page 147). SERVES 4

FOR THE CHUTNEY

1 small garlic clove, peeled

½ jalapeño pepper, seeded and inner ribs discarded

1 teaspoon peeled and coarsely chopped fresh ginger

½ cup lightly packed fresh cilantro leaves

½ cup lightly packed fresh mint leaves

¼ cup raw cashews

2 tablespoons unsweetened shredded coconut

1 tablespoon freshly squeezed lime juice

Salt

Freshly ground black pepper

¼ cup grapeseed or canola oil

STORAGE The chutney can be refrigerated for up to 1 day.

TO MAKE THE CHUTNEY

1. Fit the food processor with the *s blade*. With the motor running, drop the garlic clove and jalapeño through the feed tube to chop. Add the ginger, and process until finely chopped. Stop and scrape down the sides.

2. Add the cilantro, mint, cashews, coconut, and lime juice, and season with salt and pepper. Process to a coarse paste. Stop and scrape down the sides.

3. With the motor running, drizzle the grapeseed oil through the feed tube and process until incorporated. Season with salt and pepper. Transfer to a small bowl and cover with plastic wrap, placing the wrap directly on the surface of the chutney. Refrigerate until ready to use.

FOR THE CHOPS

2 large garlic cloves, peeled

1 tablespoon peeled and coarsely chopped fresh ginger

2 scallions, coarsely chopped

½ cup low-sodium, gluten-free tamari or soy sauce

1 tablespoon toasted sesame oil

1 tablespoon Asian fish sauce

2 tablespoons honey

¼ cup grapeseed or vegetable oil

4 (¾-inch to 1-inch-thick) bone-in pork chops

Kosher salt

Freshly ground black pepper

Vegetable oil, for oiling

INGREDIENT INFO For this recipe, you want to buy nice, thick pork chops because thin chops will dry out. If you're able to find them, pork chops from heritage breeds are typically more flavorful and juicy than conventional chops.

TO MAKE THE CHOPS

1. Fit the mini food processor with the *s blade*. Add the garlic, ginger, and scallions. Process until finely chopped. Stop and scrape down the sides. Add the tamari, sesame oil, fish sauce, honey, and grapeseed oil. Process until smooth.

2. Place the pork chops in a large zip-top bag and pour the marinade over, sealing the bag and shaking to coat. Refrigerate 4 to 8 hours, turning the bag occasionally.

3. Remove the pork chops from the marinade, and pat dry. Season with salt and pepper. Let sit at room temperature for 15 minutes to an hour.

4. Preheat the grill to medium heat. Clean and oil the grill grates. Place the pork chops on the grill and cook, covered, until browned on the bottom, about 5 to 7 minutes. Turn over, reduce the heat to low, and cook, covered, until browned on the other side and cooked through, about 5 minutes. The internal temperature should read 145°F to 150°F.

5. Alternatively, sear the pork chops in a large ovenproof skillet with 2 tablespoons of vegetable oil over medium-high heat until browned on the bottom, 3 to 4 minutes. Flip the chops and transfer the skillet to a 400°F oven. Roast until cooked through, 5 to 10 minutes.

6. Transfer to a plate or cutting board, and let it rest 5 minutes before serving. Drizzle the pork chops with any juices that have accumulated, and serve with the chutney.

Coffee-Marinated Grilled Pork Tenderloin

Prep time: 10 minutes, plus 8 hours to marinate, and 15 minutes to sit

Cook time: 20 minutes

GLUTEN-FREE OPTION, NUT-FREE

This is the perfect Sunday night meal, developed one Father's Day a few years ago when I knew we'd be out all day but still wanted something special for dinner. Pork tenderloins are marinated overnight in a mixture of coffee, molasses, lime, and tamari or soy sauce, creating a caramelized crust that tastes phenomenal. The coffee marinade is also outstanding with skirt steak. Marinate it overnight, just as you would the pork. Serve this with the Curried Carrot-Coconut Brown Rice (page 115), and you'll forget all about the work week ahead. SERVES 4 TO 6

2 garlic cloves, peeled

½ jalapeño pepper, seeded and inner ribs discarded

1 tablespoon peeled and coarsely chopped fresh ginger

½ cup ground coffee (regular or decaf)

¼ cup low-sodium, gluten-free tamari or soy sauce

¼ cup maple syrup

¼ cup blackstrap molasses

½ cup extra-virgin olive oil

Zest of 1 lime

Juice of 1 lime

Kosher salt

Freshly ground black pepper

2 pork tenderloins (about 2 to 2½ pounds total), trimmed and silverskin removed (see How-to)

Vegetable oil, for oiling

1. Fit the mini food processor with the *s blade*. Add the garlic cloves, jalapeño, and ginger. Process until finely chopped. Stop and scrape down the sides.

2. Add the coffee, tamari, maple syrup, molasses, olive oil, lime zest, and lime juice, and season with salt and pepper. Process until smooth. Put the pork in a large zip-top bag, and pour the marinade over. Seal and shake the bag to coat the pork. Refrigerate for 8 to 24 hours.

3. Remove the pork from the marinade and pat dry. Let sit at room temperature for 15 minutes to an hour. Season with salt and pepper.

4. Preheat the grill to medium high. Clean and oil the grill grates. Put the tenderloins on the grill, and reduce the heat to medium. Cover and cook for 8 to 10 minutes, until browned on the bottom. Flip and cook for another 8 to 10 minutes, or until an instant-read thermometer inserted into the thickest part reads 145°F.

5. Alternatively, sear the tenderloins in a large ovenproof skillet with 2 tablespoons of vegetable oil over medium-high heat until browned on all sides, turning occasionally, about 7 minutes total. Transfer the skillet to a 425°F oven, and roast until cooked through, 10 to 15 minutes.

6. Transfer to a cutting board, and let it rest for 10 minutes. Slice the pork, drizzle with any accumulated juices, and serve.

HOW-TO Silverskin is a thin, pearlescent membrane that runs along certain cuts of meat. It doesn't break down when cooked but instead becomes tough and chewy. To trim it, slide your knife underneath a small portion of the membrane, releasing it from the meat. Grip the membrane with one hand and peel it back while using the other hand to swipe between the meat and the membrane with a sharp knife. For the best results, swipe your knife at a slight upward angle, removing as little meat as possible.

Vegetarian & Vegan Dinners

Red and Green Veggie Pizzas

Prep time: 20 minutes • Cook time: 10 minutes

VEGETARIAN

If my five-year-old could, she would eat pizza every day, probably for every meal. These veggie pizzas are a family favorite. She gets pizza, and I get her to eat some vegetables—it's a win-win. You could certainly do just red sauce or just green sauce, but it's fun to make several pizzas and have both. Get creative and experiment with other veggies, according to what you have or like. MAKES 4 (9-INCH) PIZZAS

1 small or ½ medium yellow summer squash, trimmed

1 small or ½ medium zucchini, trimmed

4 ounces cremini or white button mushrooms, trimmed

¼ small red onion

Pizza Dough (page 75)

Flour, for flouring

Roasted Tomato Sauce (page 41)

Pesto (page 36) or Vegan Pesto (page 37)

1 pound thinly sliced fresh mozzarella cheese

2 to 4 ounces goat cheese (optional)

Salt

Freshly ground black pepper

Extra-virgin olive oil, for drizzling

Grated Parmesan cheese, for serving

2 to 3 cups arugula, for serving (optional)

1. Preheat the oven to 500°F. If you have a pizza stone, place it on the bottom rack of the oven (let it preheat for an hour, if you have the time). Line a rimless baking sheet with parchment paper.

2. Fit the food processor with the *slicing disc.* Push the yellow squash through the feed tube to slice. Repeat with the zucchini, mushrooms, and onion. Transfer the vegetables to a large bowl, and toss to combine.

3. Lightly flour a work surface. Working with one piece of pizza dough at a time, flatten it into a ½-inch-thick round. Using a rolling pin, roll the dough into a 9-inch round. Transfer to the parchment-lined baking sheet, and top with either the tomato sauce or pesto. Arrange a few slices of mozzarella and some crumbled goat cheese (if using) on top, followed by some of the vegetables. It's best to top sparingly to avoid a soggy crust. Sprinkle the pizza with salt and pepper, and drizzle with a touch of olive oil.

4. Slide the pizza (on the parchment) onto a pizza stone, or bake the pizza directly on the baking sheet on the lowest rack of the oven until the crust is golden, 5 to 8 minutes for the pizza stone and 8 to 12 minutes for the baking sheet. Transfer to a cutting board, and sprinkle with Parmesan cheese and arugula, if using. Drizzle with a bit more olive oil.

5. Repeat steps 3 and 4 with the remaining pieces of dough. Cut into wedges, and serve.

HOW-TO If you have a pizza stone, now's the time to use it. If not, no worries—you can bake the pizzas on a baking sheet. Just be sure to bake them on the lowest rack of the oven to achieve a crispy crust. If you make a lot of pizza, though, it's worth investing in a pizza stone. It will yield a crispier, more evenly cooked crust. I use parchment paper to transfer the pizza to the stone (I cook the pizza right on the parchment). Once it's cooked, use tongs to slide the pizza and parchment out onto a cutting board.

Linguini with Spinach and Ricotta-Walnut Pesto

Prep time: 10 minutes • Cook time: 10 minutes

GLUTEN-FREE OPTION, VEGETARIAN

The pesto for this recipe is one of the simplest but most luxurious of no-cook pasta sauces. When tossed with hot linguini and spinach, the sauce turns creamy and rich. And did I mention that the sauce can be thrown together in the time it takes to bring a pot of water to a boil? Like all the pasta recipes in this chapter, simply choose a gluten-free commercial pasta if gluten is a problem in your home. SERVES 4 TO 6

1 garlic clove, peeled

½ cup lightly packed fresh parsley leaves

½ cup walnuts

1 teaspoon lemon zest

1 cup ricotta cheese

¼ cup grated Parmesan cheese

2 tablespoons extra-virgin olive oil

Kosher salt

Freshly ground black pepper

1 pound linguini, regular or gluten-free

3 cups packed baby spinach leaves (about 5 ounces)

1 lemon, halved

1. Bring a large pot of water to a boil.

2. In the meantime, make the pesto. Fit the food processor with the *s blade*. With the motor running, drop the garlic clove through the feed tube to chop. Add the parsley, and process until chopped. Stop and scrape down the sides.

3. Add the walnuts and lemon zest. Process until the walnuts are finely chopped. Scrape the mixture into a large bowl, and stir in the ricotta, Parmesan, and olive oil. Season with salt and pepper.

4. When the water boils, salt it generously and add the pasta. Cook according to the package directions until 1 minute before it's al dente (firm to the bite). Ladle out 1 cup of the pasta water, and set aside. Add the spinach, and stir to wilt.

5. Drain the pasta and spinach, and immediately transfer them to the bowl with the pesto. Add ½ cup of the pasta water, and squeeze in the juice of ½ lemon. Season generously with salt and pepper. Toss well to coat. Add more pasta water or lemon juice as needed. Divide the linguini among serving bowls, and serve immediately.

INGREDIENT INFO When it comes to ricotta, in this recipe you want to use the best quality you can find. I'm lucky to have an Italian market near me where I can buy the super-fresh stuff (the kind that comes in a tin with a big mound on the top), but if you buy ricotta from the grocery store, just be sure to seek out brands with no preservatives, gums, or fillers.

Pasta with Roasted Red Pepper Pesto and Crispy Kale

Prep time: 20 minutes • Cook time: 30 minutes

GLUTEN-FREE OPTION, VEGETARIAN

This pesto is one of the only ways I can get my five-year-old to eat red peppers. The pesto is slightly sweet, smoky, and garlicky, and yet it tastes mild when tossed with pasta. (It's also great over grilled fish, chicken, or steak, or even slathered on grilled cheese sandwiches.) To add serious flavor and texture, I top each bowl with a mound of kale chips. SERVES 6

FOR THE KALE

1 large bunch lacinato kale (about 1 pound), stems removed and discarded (see Ingredient info, page 199)

2 tablespoons extra-virgin olive oil

¼ cup freshly grated Parmesan cheese

½ teaspoon lemon zest

Kosher salt

Freshly ground black pepper

FOR THE PESTO

4 tablespoons extra-virgin olive oil, divided, plus more for brushing

2 large red bell peppers, halved, seeded, and inner ribs discarded

2 garlic cloves, peeled

2 tablespoons toasted pine nuts (see How-to, page 37)

½ cup packed fresh basil leaves *or* ¼ cup packed fresh basil leaves and ¼ cup packed fresh mint leaves

½ cup grated Parmesan cheese, divided

¼ teaspoon red pepper flakes (optional)

Juice of ½ lemon, plus more for seasoning

Kosher salt

Freshly ground black pepper

1 pound rotini, fusilli, or similar pasta (regular or gluten-free)

TO MAKE THE KALE

1. Preheat the oven to 375°F. Line 2 large baking sheets with parchment paper.

2. Tear the kale leaves into bite-size pieces, and arrange them on paper towels. Pat the leaves dry.

3. In a large bowl, toss the kale with the olive oil to thoroughly coat. Add the Parmesan cheese and lemon zest, and season with salt and pepper. Toss to coat.

4. Spread the kale on the baking sheets in a single layer. Bake for 15 to 17 minutes, turning the pans 180 degrees halfway through, until the kale is crispy. Let sit at room temperature until needed, up to several hours.

TO MAKE THE PESTO

1. Preheat the broiler to high, and place a rack 5 to 6 inches from the heating element. Line a baking sheet with foil, and brush it lightly with oil.

2. Arrange the peppers, cut-side down, on the baking sheet. Broil until blackened, about 10 minutes. Cover with foil, and let steam for 10 minutes. Remove and discard the skins and stems from the peppers. Coarsely chop.

3. Fit the food processor with the *s blade*. With the motor running, drop the garlic cloves through the feed tube to chop. Add the roasted red peppers, pine nuts, basil, ¼ cup of Parmesan cheese, red pepper flakes (if using), lemon juice, and a generous pinch of salt and pepper. Process to a coarse paste. Stop and scrape down the sides.

4. With the motor running, drizzle 2 table-spoons of olive oil through the feed tube to incorporate. Taste and season with additional salt, pepper, and lemon juice as needed.

5. Bring a large pot of salted water to a boil. Cook the pasta to al dente (firm to the bite) according to the package directions. Before draining, ladle off ½ cup of the pasta water.

6. Drain the pasta, and transfer it back to the pot. Stir in the red pepper pesto and the reserved pasta water, and toss to coat. Add the remaining 2 tablespoons of olive oil and ¼ cup of Parmesan, and season with salt and pepper. Stir to combine.

7. Serve the pasta in shallow bowls, and top with the crispy kale.

INGREDIENT INFO Lacinato kale is also known by many other names, including Tuscan kale, dinosaur kale, and black kale. It has dark green leaves that are more tender than their curly brethren. To cut out the stems, fold the leaves in half like a book, then run your knife down along the side of the stem to remove it.

STORAGE The pesto can be refrigerated for up to 2 days. Place a piece of plastic wrap directly on the surface before refrigerating. The kale chips can be stored at room temperature for up to 1 day.

Penne Pasta with Kale Pesto and Roasted Grape Tomatoes

Prep time: 30 minutes • Cook time: 30 minutes

GLUTEN-FREE OPTION, VEGETARIAN

We call kale pesto "green sauce" in our house, and it's a weeknight staple. Not only is it delicious, but it's one of the only vegetable variations that I can always count on my five-year-old to devour. Who wouldn't love kale cocooned in pine nuts, Parmesan cheese, and extra-virgin olive oil? Sweet roasted grape tomatoes are the perfect counterpoint to the salty, slightly bitter pesto. SERVES 4 TO 6

FOR THE PESTO

2 garlic cloves, peeled

4 cups packed coarsely chopped lacinato
    kale leaves, stems removed and discarded
    (about 1 bunch)

⅓ cup toasted pine nuts (see How-to, page 37)

½ cup freshly grated Parmesan cheese

Kosher salt

Freshly ground black pepper

1 tablespoon freshly squeezed lemon juice

2 tablespoons water

¼ cup good-quality extra-virgin olive oil

FOR THE PASTA

2 pints grape tomatoes

2 tablespoons extra-virgin olive oil

Kosher salt

Freshly ground black pepper

Pinch of sugar (optional)

1 pound penne pasta (regular, whole-wheat,
    or gluten-free)

1 tablespoon butter

Handful freshly grated Parmesan cheese,
    plus more for serving

TO MAKE THE PESTO

1. Fit the food processor with the *s blade*. With the motor running, drop the garlic cloves through the feed tube to chop.

2. Add the kale, pine nuts, and Parmesan cheese, and season with salt and pepper. Process until coarsely chopped, stopping and scraping down the sides as needed. Add the lemon juice and water. Process to a paste.

3. With the motor running, slowly drizzle the olive oil through the feed tube to incorporate. Taste and season with additional salt, pepper, and lemon juice as needed.

TO MAKE THE PASTA

1. Preheat the oven to 400°F.

2. Spread the tomatoes out on a baking sheet, and drizzle with the olive oil. Season generously with salt and pepper, and toss to coat. If the tomatoes aren't very sweet, sprinkle them with a pinch of sugar. Roast until the tomatoes start to pop and collapse, stirring once or twice, 18 to 20 minutes. Let sit at room temperature until ready to use, up to 4 hours.

3. In the meantime, bring a large pot of water to a boil. Season with salt. Cook the pasta to al dente (firm to the bite) according to the package directions. Before draining, ladle off 1 cup of the pasta water and reserve.

4. Drain the pasta, and transfer it back to the pot. Add the butter and ¾ cup of the kale pesto. Place the pot over medium-low heat, and toss to coat. Add ¼ to ½ cup of the pasta water to create a smooth sauce. Fold in the tomatoes with any juices that have accumulated in the pan.

5. Remove the pot from the heat, add a handful of freshly grated Parmesan cheese, and season with salt and pepper. If the pasta looks dry, add another splash of the pasta water.

6. Divide the pasta into bowls, garnish with a bit more Parmesan, and serve.

STORAGE The kale pesto can be refrigerated for up to 3 days. Drizzle a bit of olive oil over the top before refrigerating.

Fondue and Fixings

Prep time: 10 minutes • Cook time: 10 minutes

NUT-FREE, VEGETARIAN

You know those nights when the kids are being super "needy" (read, whiny), you're tired, and you just want to get dinner on the table with some modicum of peace? Make fondue. It is dead simple, incredibly quick, and kids love it. So do adults. Dipping food in warm, gooey cheese—how fun and delicious is that? This is my go-to fondue recipe, which comes together in no time thanks to the shredding power of the food processor. Serve it with good bread, steamed vegetables, and crisp green apple slices, and you've got a wholesome dinner. SERVES 4

1 pound Comté, Gruyère, and Emmentaler cheese (use one or a mix)

2 tablespoons cornstarch

1 garlic clove, peeled and halved

1 cup plus 2 tablespoons dry white wine

Freshly ground black pepper

French bread torn into bite-size pieces, for serving

Steamed vegetables, such as small potatoes, cauliflower, and broccoli florets, for serving

Green apple slices, for serving

INGREDIENT INFO Comté is similar to Gruyère but has a sweeter, nuttier flavor and is perfect for fondue. It's produced in the Jura Mountain region of eastern France from cows that graze on the region's lush pastureland. It's available at most cheese shops and supermarkets.

1. Fit the food processor with the *shredding disc*. Push the cheese through the feed tube to shred. Transfer to a medium bowl, and toss with the cornstarch.

2. Rub the inside of a fondue pot with the cut sides of the garlic. Discard the garlic. Add the wine, and bring to a boil.

3. Reduce the heat to medium low. Add a quarter of the shredded cheese, and stir until melted. Continue stirring in the cheese, a quarter at a time, until melted. Cook, stirring, until the fondue is completely smooth and richly coats the back of a spoon. Season with pepper.

4. Serve the hot fondue with crusty bread, steamed vegetables, and apple slices for dipping.

Chilled Peanut Soba Noodles with Spinach and Cucumber

Prep time: 15 minutes, plus 1 hour to chill

GLUTEN-FREE OPTION, VEGETARIAN

I love soba noodles, which are made from buckwheat and have a nutty flavor, but you can swap in spaghetti or do a mix of half soba and half spaghetti. The noodles can be tossed in the sauce up to a day ahead, and the salad portion can be folded in right before serving. For a peanut-free version, use almond or cashew butter and chopped toasted cashews. By the way, mirin is a kind of rice wine, similar to sake but with less alcohol. SERVES 6 TO 8

2 large garlic cloves, peeled

½ cup natural creamy peanut butter

½ cup low-sodium, gluten-free tamari or soy sauce

¼ cup mirin

2 tablespoons rice vinegar

3 tablespoons honey

½ teaspoon sriracha, plus more for serving

1 teaspoon toasted sesame oil

2 teaspoons freshly squeezed lime juice

¼ cup grapeseed or canola oil

1 pound soba noodles or spaghetti

3 scallions, thinly sliced

2 cups thinly sliced seedless (English) cucumber

3 cups packed baby spinach leaves (about 5 ounces)

½ cup coarsely chopped fresh mint leaves

½ cup roasted peanuts

Kosher salt

Freshly ground black pepper

HOW-TO I recommend cooking the noodles in unsalted water. After the noodles have been tossed with the sauce and vegetables, take a taste. If you want more salt at that point, go for it.

1. Fit the food processor with the *s blade*. With the motor running, drop the garlic cloves through the feed tube to chop. Stop and scrape down the sides.

2. Add the peanut butter, tamari, mirin, rice vinegar, honey, sriracha, sesame oil, and lime juice. Process until smooth.

3. With the motor running, drizzle the grapeseed oil through the feed tube to incorporate.

4. In a large pot of unsalted boiling water, cook the noodles according to the package directions. Stir often at the beginning to keep them from clumping. Drain, rinse, and transfer to a large bowl. Pour the sauce over the warm noodles, and toss to combine. Refrigerate for 1 to 24 hours.

5. Add the scallions, cucumber, spinach, mint, and peanuts just before serving. Toss to coat. Taste and season with **salt and pepper** as desired. Serve with sriracha for drizzling.

Quinoa and White Bean Burgers

Prep time: 15 minutes • Cook time: 30 minutes

GLUTEN-FREE OPTION, NUT-FREE, VEGAN

These quinoa burgers are the perfect meal to make when the crisper drawer starts to run dry. The burgers are brimming with flavor, but best of all, they can be adapted to what you have on hand—swap out the scallions for shallots, switch basil or parsley for the cilantro, or sub in lime zest for the lemon zest. You get the picture. I love these burgers over a bed of greens with a smear of hummus and smashed avocado, while my husband prefers them in pita bread with a dollop of yogurt, avocado, feta cheese, and tomato. SERVES 6

½ cup red or white quinoa

Kosher salt

2 large garlic cloves, peeled

1 (15-ounce) can cannellini or navy beans, drained and rinsed

3 scallions, coarsely chopped

¼ cup lightly packed fresh cilantro leaves

1 teaspoon lemon zest

1 teaspoon ground cumin

Freshly ground black pepper

½ cup defrosted frozen peas

½ cup panko bread crumbs (regular or gluten-free)

3 tablespoons extra-virgin olive oil, divided

Toppings for serving, such as hummus, smashed avocado, and sliced tomatoes (and plain Greek yogurt and feta cheese if not vegan)

Pita bread, buns, or greens, for serving (optional)

1. Rinse the quinoa in cold water, and drain. In a small saucepan, cover the quinoa with 1 inch of cold water. Add a pinch of salt. Bring to a boil. Reduce to a simmer; cover and cook for 16 to 18 minutes, or until most of the grains have unfurled like little curlicues. Drain and let cool.

2. Fit the food processor with the *s blade*. With the motor running, drop the garlic cloves through the feed tube to chop. Add the beans, scallions, cilantro, lemon zest, and cumin, and season with salt and pepper. Process until the mixture forms a coarse purée, stopping and scraping down the sides.

3. Add the quinoa; pulse until a coarse paste forms. Taste and season with additional salt or pepper as needed.

4. Transfer to a bowl, and stir in the peas and bread crumbs. Form the mixture into 6 patties, and place them on a piece of wax or parchment paper.

5. In a large cast iron or nonstick skillet over medium-high heat, heat 2 tablespoons of olive oil. Add the burgers, and cook until golden brown on the bottom, about 5 minutes. Flip the burgers, add the remaining 1 tablespoon of olive oil, and cook until golden on the other side, 3 to 5 minutes longer.

6. Serve the burgers with the toppings of your choice either in pita bread, on buns, or over greens.

STORAGE The uncooked burgers can be covered and refrigerated for up to 1 day before cooking.

TIME SAVER Whenever I make a batch of grains (quinoa, brown rice, millet, or others), I always make extra to either use later in the week or freeze for quick dinners down the line. These burgers are a great use for leftover quinoa—you'll need 2 cups of cooked quinoa for the recipe.

Black Bean Veggie Burgers

Prep time: 20 minutes • Cook time: 10 minutes

GLUTEN-FREE OPTION, NUT-FREE, VEGAN

The term "veggie burger" always reminds me of my college days, when I survived on frozen, flavorless burgers that took minutes to heat up. Luckily, these are a far cry from those processed hockey puck patties of my youth. I'll often make a double batch and freeze half for another night—it's like college all over again, just miles more delicious. Serve the burgers on buns with your favorite toppings. I go for mayonnaise, smashed avocado, and tomato, and my five-year-old prefers Cheddar cheese and ketchup. SERVES 4

½ small sweet potato, peeled

1 small beet, peeled

½ cup old-fashioned rolled oats (regular or gluten-free)

2 garlic cloves, peeled

2 scallions, coarsely chopped

1 (15-ounce) can black beans, drained and rinsed

1 tablespoon tahini

1 teaspoon ground cumin

1 teaspoon ground coriander

½ teaspoon dried oregano

Kosher salt

Freshly ground black pepper

2 tablespoons extra-virgin olive oil

Burger buns and fixings, for serving

1. Fit the food processor with the *shredding disc*. Push the sweet potato and beet through the feed tube to shred. Transfer to a large bowl.

2. Refit the food processor with the *s blade* (no need to wash). Add the oats, and process to a coarse flour. Add to the vegetables.

3. Reassemble the food processor with the *s blade* (no need to wash). With the motor running, drop the garlic cloves through the feed tube to chop. Add the scallions, and process to chop. Stop and scrape down the sides.

4. Add the black beans, tahini, cumin, coriander, and oregano, and season generously with salt and pepper. Pulse until everything is incorporated, about 8 pulses. Stop and scrape down the sides.

5. Add the shredded vegetables and ground oats to the processor, and season again with salt and pepper. Pulse until everything is incorporated, about 15 pulses. Form the mixture into 4 (½-inch-thick) patties.

6. In a large nonstick skillet over medium-high heat, heat the olive oil. Add the burgers and cook, covered, until lightly browned and crisp on the bottom, 3 to 4 minutes. Flip and cook, covered, until browned on the other side, 2 to 4 minutes. Serve with your favorite burger fixings.

STORAGE The uncooked burger patties can be refrigerated for up to 1 day. The cooked burgers can be frozen for up to 2 months, separated by pieces of parchment or wax paper. Defrost in the microwave or at room temperature, and reheat in a toaster oven.

Falafel

Prep time: 10 minutes, plus 24 hours to soak • Cook time: 20 minutes

GLUTEN-FREE, NUT-FREE, VEGAN

When my husband and I moved to the Hudson Valley several years ago, one of the things we missed most about city living was access to ethnic food. Falafel ranked high on the list, and I was left with no other option but to start making it from scratch. Luckily, I discovered it's not hard at all, especially since the mixture comes together in less than 10 minutes in the food processor. These light and crispy little balls are brimming with fresh herbs, garlic, and spices. Believe it or not, they're even better than the ones we used to get in the city. You'll never miss take-out again. SERVES 4 TO 6

2 cups dried chickpeas

4 garlic cloves, peeled

1 small onion, coarsely chopped

½ cup lightly packed fresh parsley leaves

½ cup lightly packed fresh cilantro leaves

1 tablespoon ground cumin

1½ teaspoons ground coriander

¾ teaspoon ground cayenne pepper

1 tablespoon kosher salt

1 teaspoon baking powder

Grapeseed or canola oil, for frying

Tahini Sauce (page 40), for serving (optional)

1. In a large bowl, cover the chickpeas with 3 inches of water. Let sit at room temperature for 24 hours, until at least doubled in size. You may need to add more water to keep the beans covered. Drain and rinse.

2. Fit the food processor with the *s blade*. With the motor running, drop the garlic cloves through the feed tube to chop. Add the chickpeas, onion, parsley, cilantro, cumin, coriander, cayenne, salt, and baking powder. Pulse until finely minced and sticky, but not puréed, stopping and scraping down the sides occasionally, about 80 pulses. The mixture should hold together when pinched but should still be slightly crumbly. Taste and add additional salt or seasonings, if desired.

3. Line a large baking sheet with paper towels.

4. In a large, heavy-bottomed saucepan, heat 3 inches of oil over medium-high heat to 350°F. It will shimmer, and a crumb of falafel will bubble and float back to the surface if tossed in.

5. Scooping out heaping tablespoons of falafel at a time, form the mixture into small balls. Carefully slide a few of the falafel balls into the hot oil, making sure not to overcrowd the pot. Cook until evenly golden brown, stirring occasionally, about 2 minutes.

6. Using a slotted spoon, transfer the falafel to the paper towel-lined baking sheet to drain. Season with salt. Repeat with the remaining falafel. Serve warm or at room temperature with Tahini Sauce for dipping (if using).

STORAGE The uncooked falafel mixture can be made up to 3 days in advance. Store it in an airtight container in the refrigerator until you're ready to cook. From there, fresh falafel are just a quick fry away!

Curried Chickpea Salad Wraps

Prep time: 15 minutes, plus 30 minutes to chill

GLUTEN-FREE OPTION, VEGETARIAN

This dish takes only 15 minutes to prepare, and it makes a big batch that we use for lunches throughout the week (it's even better the next day). The food processor takes all the work out of having to finely chop vegetables and aromatics. With mango chutney and dried currants for sweetness, curry powder for spice, lime juice for acidity, roasted cashews for crunch, and a bit of creamy mayonnaise to bind everything together, the salad hits all the right marks of flavor and texture. SERVES 6

1 large garlic clove, peeled

1 large scallion, coarsely chopped

1 medium carrot, coarsely chopped

1 medium celery stalk, coarsely chopped

¼ cup lightly packed, coarsely chopped fresh cilantro

2 (15-ounce) cans chickpeas, drained and rinsed

¼ cup mayonnaise

2 tablespoons mango chutney

Juice of ½ lime

1 teaspoon curry powder

3 tablespoons dried currants

¼ cup coarsely chopped toasted cashews (see How-to, page 37)

Salt

Freshly ground black pepper

Whole-wheat tortillas or collard green leaves, for serving

Avocado slices, for serving

1. Fit the food processor with the *s blade*. With the motor running, drop the garlic through the feed tube to chop. Add the scallion, carrot, celery, and cilantro. Pulse until finely chopped.

2. Add the chickpeas, and pulse until they are slightly broken up and distributed throughout the vegetables, about 10 pulses.

3. Transfer the mixture to a large bowl, and add the mayonnaise, mango chutney, lime juice, curry powder, currants, and cashews. Season with salt and pepper, and toss well to coat. Taste and season with additional salt or pepper as needed.

4. Refrigerate the salad for 30 minutes to allow the flavors to meld.

5. Pile the chickpea salad onto whole-wheat tortillas or collard green leaves, and top with a few slices of avocado. Wrap and serve.

SIMPLE SWAP For a slight variation, try roasted peanuts instead of the cashews. For a nut-free version, you can omit the cashews altogether. To make this a vegan dish, simply substitute Vegenaise for the mayo. Skip the tortillas if you're gluten-free; collard greens or a large-leaf variety of lettuce make great wraps instead.

STORAGE The chickpea salad, minus the wrappers, can be stored in the refrigerator for up to 5 days.

Sweet Potato and Brussels Sprouts Hash with Fried Eggs

Prep time: 15 minutes • Cook time: 20 minutes

GLUTEN-FREE, VEGETARIAN

Sweet, salty, and crunchy with an oozing egg on top? Sign me up. This hash has a touch of maple syrup for sweetness, a subtle kick of spice from red pepper flakes, and crunch from chopped pecans. Although it's pretty amazing on its own (it makes for a great vegan side dish), a fried egg takes it over the top. For a spicier hash, feel free to up the amount of red pepper flakes (or you can omit them altogether if you're serving kids or prefer a milder version). You'll need a 12-inch nonstick skillet with a lid for this dish. SERVES 4

2 cups Brussels sprouts (about 8 ounces)

1 large sweet potato (about 1 pound), peeled

¼ cup plus 2 tablespoons extra-virgin olive oil, divided

1 large leek, white and light green parts only, halved and thinly sliced crosswise

1 large garlic clove, thinly sliced

Kosher salt

Freshly ground black pepper

1 teaspoon finely chopped fresh thyme

1 tablespoon freshly squeezed lemon juice

1 tablespoon maple syrup

⅓ cup coarsely chopped toasted pecans (see How-to, page 37)

¼ teaspoon red pepper flakes

4 large eggs

Shaved Parmesan cheese, for serving (optional)

1. Remove and discard the tough outer leaves of the Brussels sprouts. Trim off the brown bottoms.

2. Fit the food processor with the *shredding disc*. Push the sweet potato and Brussels sprouts through the feed tube to shred.

3. In a 12-inch nonstick skillet over medium-low heat, heat ¼ cup of olive oil. Add the leek and garlic, and season with salt and pepper. Cover and cook, stirring occasionally, until the leeks are softened and starting to brown, about 5 to 6 minutes.

4. Stir in the thyme and the shredded sweet potatoes and Brussels sprouts, and season with salt and pepper. Spread the vegetables in an even layer. Cover and cook for 6 to 8 minutes, or until the bottom is nicely browned. Then stir well, scraping up any browned bits from the bottom of the pan, and spread the vegetables in an even layer again.

5. Cover and cook about 3 minutes longer, or until the vegetables are browned and tender. Stir well, scraping up the bits from the bottom of the pan. Remove the pan from the heat, and stir in the lemon juice, maple syrup, pecans, and red pepper flakes. Taste and season generously with salt and pepper.

6. In a large nonstick skillet over medium heat, heat the remaining 2 tablespoons of olive oil (if you only have one nonstick skillet, transfer the hash to 4 serving bowls and wipe out the pan). Crack the eggs into the hot skillet. After about 1 minute, when the outer edges of the eggs turn white, cover the pan and lower the heat to medium low. Cook for 3 to 4 minutes, or until the whites are cooked but the yolks are still runny. Season with salt and pepper.

7. Divide the hash among 4 shallow bowls, and top each with a fried egg. Using a vegetable peeler, shave a few slices of Parmesan cheese over each bowl, if you'd like, and serve.

HOW-TO Have you ever found yourself scrambling to get the spices measured before what you're cooking burns? Don't worry; me too. It's easier to measure out the spices at the beginning and place them in a small bowl. That way, they'll be ready to go when you need them. If you do find yourself in a scramble, simply remove the pot from the heat while you rummage through your spice cabinet.

Desserts

Almond-Cherry Thumbprint Cookies

Prep time: 15 minutes, plus 15 minutes to chill • Cook time: 15 minutes

GLUTEN-FREE, VEGETARIAN

These irresistible almond thumbprint cookies are perfect for holiday cookie tins. Made with almond flour (sometimes called almond meal), they're naturally gluten-free, with a wonderful almond flavor that's enhanced by a dab of cherry jam, although you can use any jam flavor you like. The idea for the recipe came from my friend and cookbook author Samantha Seneviratne, who makes a stellar hazelnut thumbprint cookie (try swapping the almond flour for hazelnut flour!). You won't believe how quickly the dough comes together in the food processor, making this one of the easiest cookie recipes ever. MAKES 25 TO 30 COOKIES

8 tablespoons unsalted butter, at room temperature

½ cup confectioners' sugar

½ teaspoon ground cinnamon

¼ teaspoon kosher salt

½ teaspoon almond extract

2 egg yolks

2 cups almond flour

¼ cup cherry jam (or flavor of your choice)

1. Preheat the oven to 350°F. Line 2 baking sheets with parchment paper.

2. Fit the food processor with the *s blade*. Add the butter, sugar, cinnamon, salt, almond extract, and egg yolks. Process until smooth, stopping and scraping down the sides occasionally. Add the almond flour, and pulse until combined, 10 to 12 pulses.

3. Remove the blade, and stir the dough with a rubber spatula. Using two spoons or a mini ice cream scoop, scoop out 1-inch balls of the dough, and place them about 2 inches apart on the baking sheets. If you're using two spoons, roll the dough into balls. Refrigerate the baking sheets for 15 to 30 minutes to chill.

4. Using a damp finger, make an indentation in the center of each cookie. Fill each indentation with about ¼ to ½ teaspoon of jam. Bake for 14 to 16 minutes, turning the pans 180 degrees halfway through, or until the cookies are golden around the edges. Cool the cookies on the baking sheets set on wire racks, and serve.

STORAGE The cookies can be refrigerated for up to 1 week.

TIME SAVER A mini ice cream scoop is the perfect tool for scooping out cookie dough. It takes all the grunt work (and mess!) out of scooping dough with two spoons, and it makes the task go much faster.

Lemon Bars with Graham Cracker Crust and Whipped Cream

Prep time: 20 minutes, plus 1½ hours to cool • Cook time: 30 minutes

NUT-FREE, VEGETARIAN

With a crisp graham cracker crust, a layer of rich lemon filling, and a crown of creamy whipped cream, this dessert satisfies everyone. I surprised my daughter with a batch of these bars on her first day of kindergarten, and they instantly became one of her favorite desserts. Best of all, they can be made ahead of time, making them perfect for potlucks and showers. MAKES 9 BARS

2 cups Graham Cracker Pie Dough (page 78)

1 (14-ounce) can sweetened condensed milk

2 egg yolks

½ teaspoon lemon zest

½ cup freshly squeezed lemon juice

1 cup cold heavy (whipping) cream

1 tablespoon sugar

1 teaspoon vanilla extract

1. Preheat the oven to 350°F.

2. Spread the Graham Cracker Pie Dough in an 8-by-8-inch square baking dish. Using your fingers and the bottom of a flat measuring cup, press the dough evenly over the bottom and sides of the pan, going 1½ inches up the sides. Bake the crust for 10 to 15 minutes, or until light golden and fragrant. Let cool on a wire rack for at least 30 minutes.

3. Fit the mini food processor with the *s blade*. Add the sweetened condensed milk and egg yolks. Process until smooth. Add the lemon zest and lemon juice, and process until incorporated. Pour the filling into the cooled crust. Spread it to the edges, and smooth the top. Bake for 15 minutes, or until set. Let cool in the pan on a wire rack.

4. To make the whipped cream, fit the food processor (standard size) with the *s blade*. Add the heavy cream, sugar, and vanilla. Process for 20 to 30 seconds, until thickened. Stop and scrape down the sides, and pulse 10 to 15 times, until the cream has soft, thick peaks—be sure not to overmix, or the cream could curdle. Remove the blade, and stir gently with a rubber spatula. Spread the whipped cream over the cooled lemon filling. Cover and refrigerate for at least 1 hour, or up to 1 day.

5. Cut into 9 square bars, wiping the knife with a damp towel between each cut, and serve.

STORAGE The lemon bars can be covered and refrigerated for up to 1 day.

HOW-TO Whipped cream in the food processor? Yes! Cold cream goes into the work bowl with the sugar and vanilla, and in less than a minute, you get the smoothest, creamiest whipped cream you can imagine.

Watermelon and Mint Shaved Ice

Prep time: 10 minutes, plus 6 hours to freeze

GLUTEN-FREE, NUT-FREE, VEGAN

Shaved ice (also known as granita) is typically a bit of a chore to make, because you have to continuously scrape the base as it freezes to create ice flakes. This version uses the food processor instead. Watermelon is puréed with mint and lime and then frozen in ice cube trays—no scraping required! The ice cubes are then blitzed in the food processor until they become flaky, like watermelon slush. I highly suggest serving it with a dollop of lightly sweetened whipped cream. It's the perfect ending to a summertime meal. SERVES 6

4 cups 1-inch cubes seedless watermelon
⅓ cup sugar
1 tablespoon freshly squeezed lime juice
2 tablespoons packed fresh mint leaves

STORAGE The watermelon ice cubes can be transferred to a large zip-top bag and frozen for up to 1 week. The shaved ice can be stored overnight in a sealed container in the freezer. Before serving, break it up with a fork.

SIMPLE SWAP Try this recipe using other melon varieties such as cantaloupe or honeydew.

1. Fit the food processor with the *s blade*. Add the watermelon, sugar, lime juice, and mint. Process until smooth. Pour the mixture into 2 ice cube trays, and freeze until firm, about 6 hours.

2. Fit the food processor with the *s blade*. Transfer the watermelon ice cubes to the food processor, and pulse, stopping and scraping down the sides occasionally, until the mixture is snowy with icy flakes, about 25 pulses. Scoop the mixture into bowls, and serve.

Frozen Banana "Ice Cream"

Prep time: 5 minutes

GLUTEN-FREE, VEGETARIAN

The first time I made this, my daughter, who was a toddler at the time, thought it was magic. Into the food processor went a few frozen bananas and a touch of milk, and out came a sweet and creamy soft-serve-style ice cream. There is something magical about this dessert. Made with just two ingredients (and no added sugar), it's healthy and yet feels indulgent. Use nut milk to make this vegan, or stick with dairy and pass up the nut toppings to make it nut-free. SERVES 4

3 large peeled frozen bananas

½ cup dairy milk or nut milk

Toppings (optional): roasted nuts, chopped chocolate, cocoa nibs, toasted coconut flakes, ground cinnamon

INGREDIENT INFO Whenever bananas start to get overripe, I peel them and toss them into a large zip-top bag that I keep in the freezer. The frozen bananas can be whizzed on a whim into ice cream and smoothies, or they can be defrosted and puréed for breads, muffins, and cakes.

1. Fit the food processor with the *s blade*. Break the frozen bananas into 2 or 3 pieces each, and place them in the processor. Process until finely chopped. Stop and scrape down the sides. With the machine running, slowly drizzle in the milk until the bananas are smooth and creamy—about the consistency of soft-serve ice cream. You might not need all the milk, or you might need a splash or two more, depending on the size of your bananas.

2. Scrape the ice cream into bowls, and sprinkle with the toppings of your choice. Serve immediately.

Sundae Supreme
Chocolate and Raspberry Sauces

Prep time: 5 minutes each • Cook time: 5 minutes each

GLUTEN-FREE, VEGETARIAN

First of all, let's talk chocolate. This is the silkiest, most luxurious chocolate sauce you could imagine, and you won't believe how easy it is. When I served it for the first time, there were literally sighs of elation at the table. While the chocolate sauce is amazing on its own, the raspberry sauce is bright and lively—a perfect partner to the rich chocolate. I use frozen raspberries, so the sauce can be made year-round. MAKES ABOUT 1¼ CUPS OF EACH SAUCE

FOR THE CHOCOLATE SAUCE

4 ounces good-quality (70% cocoa content) bittersweet chocolate

1 cup heavy (whipping) cream

1 teaspoon vanilla extract

Pinch salt

FOR THE RASPBERRY SAUCE

2 cups frozen raspberries

2 tablespoons sugar

1 teaspoon freshly squeezed lemon juice

¼ cup raspberry jam

Pinch salt

FOR SERVING

Vanilla ice cream

Chopped toasted nuts (see How-to, page 37) (optional)

Whipped cream (optional)

TO MAKE THE CHOCOLATE SAUCE

1. Fit the mini food processor with the *s blade*. Break the chocolate into small squares, and place them in the processor. Pulse until evenly chopped into small pieces, about 20 to 30 pulses. Once evenly chopped, process the chocolate until it's very finely ground.

2. In a small saucepan over high heat, bring the heavy cream, vanilla, and salt to a boil. Pour the hot cream over the chocolate in the food processor.

3. Process just until the mixture comes together and turns silky, about 5 seconds. Be careful not to overmix, as it could result in a grainy sauce. Drizzle over the dessert of your choice, and serve.

TO MAKE THE RASPBERRY SAUCE

1. In a small saucepan over medium-low heat, cook the raspberries, sugar, and lemon juice, stirring occasionally, until the raspberries have softened and released their liquid, 3 to 5 minutes.

2. Fit the mini food processor with the *s blade*. Transfer the raspberries and liquid to the processor, and add the raspberry jam and salt. Process until smooth. Serve warm or chilled with your preferred dessert.

STORAGE The sauces can be refrigerated for up to 2 weeks. To reheat, microwave on high in 15-second intervals, stirring after each, until warm.

Mango Frozen Yogurt

Prep time: 5 minutes

GLUTEN-FREE, NUT-FREE, VEGETARIAN

One day while making a mango smoothie for my daughter, I realized that if I left out the ice and liquid, I would practically have ice cream. So out came the food processor, in went frozen mangos, yogurt, honey, lime juice, and a pinch of cardamom, and within minutes I had an indulgently creamy soft-serve-style frozen yogurt with a flavor akin to a mango lassi. Needless to say, my daughter was thrilled. MAKES ABOUT 1 QUART

2 (10-ounce) bags frozen mangos

1¾ cups Greek yogurt (at least 2% fat)

¼ cup honey

¼ teaspoon ground cardamom

⅛ teaspoon kosher salt

2 teaspoons freshly squeezed lime juice

INGREDIENT INFO While I'm all for fresh produce, frozen fruit is picked at its peak of ripeness and considered a staple in my house—we use it for morning smoothies, toss it into oatmeal in the winter, and make ice cream sauce out of it. Best of all, having frozen fruit in the house means we're only 5 minutes away from homemade frozen yogurt!

1. Fit the food processor with the *s blade*. Add the mangos, yogurt, honey, cardamom, salt, and lime juice, and process until smooth, stopping and scraping down the sides occasionally.

2. Serve immediately for soft-serve-style frozen yogurt.

STORAGE I think this treat is best straight out of the food processor, but it can be frozen for up to 1 week. Just defrost it at room temperature or in the microwave in 30-second intervals until softened enough to scoop.

Chocolate–Coconut Chia Pudding

Prep time: 5 minutes, plus 4 hours to chill

GLUTEN-FREE, NUT-FREE, VEGAN

Growing up, I probably gobbled close to a thousand store-bought plastic pudding cups. I'm pretty sure it would amount to several hundred pounds of sugar. My five-year-old also has a killer sweet tooth and shares my love for all things creamy. However, instead of buying the plastic tubs, I make pudding from scratch—and I aim for more nutritious, lower-sugar treats. This pudding is sweet and luscious, but it's naturally sweetened with bananas and maple syrup. Raw cacao powder, rich in antioxidants and magnesium, gives it a rich chocolate flavor, and it's thickened with chia seeds, a fantastic source of fiber and protein. SERVES 6 TO 8

1 (13½-ounce) can coconut milk

1½ medium ripe bananas

2 tablespoons maple syrup

4 teaspoons raw cacao powder

½ teaspoon ground cinnamon

¼ teaspoon ground cardamom

¼ teaspoon kosher salt

1 teaspoon vanilla extract

¼ cup chia seeds

Toasted coconut flakes, for serving
(see How-to, page 37) (optional)

INGREDIENT INFO Long before Chia Pets, chia seeds were a staple in ancient diets, including those of the Aztecs and Mayans. Considered a superfood, they are high in omega-3 fatty acids, protein, and fiber. They also contain all of the essential amino acids required by the body. When added to liquid, they can absorb 10 times their dry weight, developing a texture similar to tapioca.

1. Fit the food processor with the *s blade*. Add the coconut milk, bananas, maple syrup, cacao powder, cinnamon, cardamom, salt, and vanilla. Process until smooth, stopping and scraping down the sides occasionally.

2. Add the chia seeds, and pulse to combine, about 5 pulses.

3. Scrape the mixture into a bowl, making sure to scrape up the chia seeds from the side of the work bowl. Cover and refrigerate for at least 4 hours or overnight.

4. Stir the pudding. Divide it into bowls, top with toasted coconut (if using), and serve.

STORAGE The pudding can be refrigerated for up to 3 days.

Vanilla Bean and Maple Yogurt with Berries and Crispy Streusel Topping

Prep time: 10 minutes · Cook time: 20 minutes

VEGETARIAN

If, like me, the streusel is your favorite part of a coffee cake or muffin, this is the recipe for you. The dough comes together in under 5 minutes in the food processor and is then pinched and squeezed into clumps—an especially great task for kids. The streusel bakes into crispy, cookie-like crumbles that are hard to resist eating straight off the pan. Luckily, it makes a big batch and freezes well, making it great for last-minute desserts. SERVES 4 (WITH LEFTOVER STREUSEL)

FOR THE STREUSEL

1 cup all-purpose flour

½ cup packed light brown sugar

¼ teaspoon ground cinnamon

¼ teaspoon kosher salt

½ cup walnuts or pecans

8 tablespoons unsalted cold butter, cut into ½-inch pieces

2 tablespoons sour cream

FOR THE YOGURT

½ vanilla bean

2 cups plain Greek yogurt

1 tablespoon maple syrup

Fresh berries or Raspberry Sauce (page 222), for serving

TO MAKE THE STREUSEL

1. Preheat the oven to 375°F. Line a baking sheet with parchment paper.

2. Fit the food processor with the *s blade*. Add the flour, brown sugar, cinnamon, and salt. Process until combined. Add the nuts, and pulse until coarsely chopped, 8 to 10 pulses. Add the cold butter, and pulse until the mixture is crumbly with pea-size pieces of butter, about 15 to 20 pulses. Add the sour cream, and pulse to incorporate, about 10 pulses.

3. Transfer the mixture to the parchment-lined baking sheet. Using your hands, pinch and squeeze the streusel to create ½-inch clumps. You're aiming for most of the mixture to be formed into clumps, with some crumbs remaining. Spread in an even layer.

4. Bake for 12 to 14 minutes, until browned along the edges and golden in the middle. Using a spatula, carefully lift up portions of the streusel and flip over, trying not to break up too many clumps. Continue flipping until all the streusel has been turned, redistributing some of the browned portions to the middle of the pan and vice versa. Bake for 5 to 6 minutes longer, or until the streusel is browned throughout. Place the pan on a cooling rack, and cool completely.

STORAGE The streusel can be stored in an airtight container at room temperature for up to 1 week or frozen for up to 2 months.

TO MAKE THE YOGURT

1. Halve the vanilla bean lengthwise, and scrape out the seeds using the back of a small knife. Stir the vanilla seeds into the yogurt. Add the maple syrup, and stir to combine.

2. To serve, layer the yogurt with fresh berries or Raspberry Sauce and streusel. I like to use tall glasses for this so that you can see the layers, but bowls work just fine. Serve with long-handled spoons.

Blueberry-Almond Galette

Prep time: 20 minutes, plus 10 minutes to chill • Cook time: 1 hour

VEGETARIAN

Growing up, my brothers and I didn't celebrate our birthdays with cake. Instead, we blew out our candles on my mom's homemade pies. Today, I'd rather eat—and bake—pie over cake any day. Blueberry is my very favorite, and this galette—a fancy name for a free-form single-crust pie— has jumped into first place. In addition to the blueberries it has a delicious almond paste on the bottom, and more almonds pressed into the outside of the crust. The result looks like something that could have come out of a French bakery. SERVES 8

FOR THE ALMOND PASTE

1 cup sliced almonds

6 tablespoons sugar

¼ teaspoon kosher salt

1 egg yolk

2 tablespoons unsalted butter, at room temperature

1 teaspoon vanilla extract

½ teaspoon almond extract

TO MAKE THE ALMOND PASTE

1. Fit the food processor with the s *blade*. Add the almonds, sugar, salt, egg yolk, butter, vanilla, and almond extract, and process until the mixture forms a paste and clumps up along the side of the work bowl.

2. Transfer to a bowl, and set aside. ➡

FOR THE PIE

3 cups blueberries

1 tablespoon cornstarch

Juice of ½ lemon

3 tablespoons sugar

½ teaspoon ground cinnamon

All-purpose flour, for flouring

½ recipe Classic Pie Dough (page 77)

1 egg, whisked

3 tablespoons sliced almonds

Vanilla ice cream, for serving (optional)

STORAGE The galette can be stored at room temperature for up to 1 day.

TO MAKE THE PIE

1. Preheat the oven to 375°F. Line a large baking sheet with parchment paper.

2. In a large bowl, toss the blueberries with the cornstarch, lemon juice, sugar, and cinnamon.

3. Lightly flour a work surface. Roll out the pie dough to ⅛-inch thickness, about 12 to 13 inches across. Transfer the dough to the baking sheet.

4. Crumble the almond paste evenly over the dough, leaving a 2-inch border. Gently press the paste into a roughly even layer— it's okay if there are a few gaps. Spread the blueberries over the almond paste.

5. Fold the pie dough over the blueberries about 2 inches in, so the center is uncovered, pinching and pleating the dough to form a rustic circle. Brush the top of the dough lightly with the beaten egg (you won't use it all), and sprinkle with the sliced almonds, pressing them so they stick to the crust. Refrigerate for 10 minutes to chill.

6. Bake until the crust is golden brown and the blueberries are bubbling around the edges, 50 to 60 minutes. Place the baking sheet on a wire rack, and let cool. Serve in wedges with a scoop of vanilla ice cream, if you wish.

Raw Cacao and Cherry-Date Nut Bars

Prep time: 10 minutes, plus 1 hour to chill

GLUTEN-FREE, VEGAN

When I decided to create a raw bar for this book, I have to admit that it was one of the recipes I was least excited about. I didn't think a date nut bar could be very exciting or satisfying. I was wrong. These bars are rich, chocolatey, chewy, and just really good. Since I'm a chocolate addict, I decided to add raw cacao powder—a superfood loaded with antioxidants, magnesium, and iron. For a nuttier depth of flavor, you can toast the cashews first, but they can also be added raw. MAKES 16 BARS

2 cups toasted or raw cashews (see How-to, page 37)

¾ cup raw cacao powder

1¼ cups unsweetened shredded coconut, divided

¼ teaspoon kosher salt

14 Medjool dates, pitted

1 cup dried cherries, or dried fruit of your choice

3 tablespoons agave nectar (or honey if not vegan)

STORAGE The bars can be wrapped individually in plastic wrap and refrigerated for up to 2 weeks or frozen for up to 3 months.

INGREDIENT INFO There are many varieties of dates (which are a tree fruit, by the way), but Medjool are considered the best. They're bigger than other varieties, with a soft flesh and an exceptional caramel-like flavor.

1. Line an 8-by-8-inch baking dish with 2 pieces of plastic wrap set crosswise, leaving plenty of overhang.

2. Fit the food processor with the *s blade*. Add the cashews, raw cacao powder, 1 cup of shredded coconut, and the salt. Process until finely chopped.

3. Add the dates, cherries, and agave. Process until the mixture comes together and forms a sticky mass, 1 to 2 minutes.

4. Scrape the mixture into the prepared pan. Using your hands, press it into a flat, even layer. Sprinkle the remaining ¼ cup of shredded coconut evenly over the top, and press to stick. Cover with the overhanging plastic wrap. Refrigerate for at least 1 hour.

5. Remove the bars from the baking dish, and unwrap. Using a sharp knife, cut into 16 bars, and serve.

Fruit Tart with Raw Macadamia Crust

Prep time: 15 to 20 minutes, plus 1 hour to chill

GLUTEN-FREE, VEGAN

A fruit tart that looks beautiful, tastes delicious, and is actually good for you? Seems too good to be true! This utterly simple but stunning tart was inspired by my friend Stanzi, who was an amazing health coach and raw foods cook. The crust is made of macadamia nuts, coconut, cinnamon, and dates. Through the magic of the food processor, they come together to form a sticky crust onto which fresh fruit and berries are arranged. MAKES 1 (9-INCH) TART

2 cups macadamia nuts

¾ cup unsweetened shredded coconut

1 teaspoon ground cinnamon

8 pitted dates, coarsely chopped

1½ teaspoons vanilla extract

2½ tablespoons extra-virgin coconut oil, melted

1 tablespoon maple syrup

½ teaspoon kosher salt

2 to 3 cups fresh fruit such as sliced strawberries, sliced kiwi, blueberries, raspberries, sliced mango, and sliced pineapple

HOW-TO No tart pan? No problem! You can simply scrape the mixture onto a serving platter and press it into a ¼-inch-thick circle about 10 inches across.

1. Fit the food processor with the *s blade*. Add the macadamias, coconut, cinnamon, dates, vanilla, coconut oil, maple syrup, and salt, and process until the nuts are finely ground and the mixture looks like wet sand. It should hold together when pinched between your fingers.

2. Scrape the mixture into a 9-inch tart pan with a removable bottom. Press it into the bottom of the pan and up the sides. Cover and refrigerate for 1 to 24 hours.

3. Before serving, arrange the fruit decoratively on the tart. Remove the sides of the pan, cut, and serve immediately.

STORAGE The tart crust can be made up to a day in advance. Cover and refrigerate.

Hazelnut-Peach Crisps

Prep time: 15 minutes · Cook time: 40 minutes

GLUTEN-FREE, VEGETARIAN

We get unbelievable peaches from our farmers' market in the summer. While it's somewhat blasphemous to eat them any way except dripping down the chin, after the fifth consecutive week of peaches, I began to wonder how I could cook them so the peach flavor would still shine. That's how these cuties were born, which I imagine as the offspring of a cookie and a fruit crisp. It's a simple, easy-to-make dessert that's perfect for all the summer stone fruits, including nectarines and apricots. SERVES 4 TO 8

Butter, for greasing

4 large ripe peaches, halved and pitted

1 cup hazelnut meal or flour

¼ teaspoon kosher salt

½ teaspoon ground cinnamon

¼ cup packed light brown sugar

4 tablespoons cold butter, cut into ½-inch pieces

1 large egg

Crème fraîche, whipped cream, or ice cream, for serving (optional)

1. Preheat the oven to 400°F. Butter a 9-inch (or approximate) baking dish.

2. Slice a thin piece off the bottom (round side) of each peach half so it sits flat. Arrange the peaches, cut-side up, in the baking dish, leaving some space between each peach.

3. Fit the mini food processor with the *s blade*. Add the hazelnut meal, salt, cinnamon, and brown sugar. Pulse to combine. Add the butter, and pulse until crumbly. Crack in the egg, and pulse until the dough comes together and sticks to the side of the bowl.

4. Pinch off pieces of the dough—about 2 tablespoons for each peach—and press the dough on top of the peaches.

5. Bake the peaches until they're soft and the topping is golden and firm to the touch, about 40 minutes, depending on how ripe your peaches are. Let cool for 10 minutes. Serve 1 to 2 peach halves per person, with a dollop of crème fraîche, whipped cream, or ice cream, if you'd like.

Apple-Pecan Crisp

Prep time: 20 minutes • Cook time: 1 hour, 5 minutes

GLUTEN-FREE OPTION, VEGETARIAN

A good crisp is a humble dessert—all brown and bumpy and crunchy and as welcome on a Tuesday night as it is on a holiday table. In this version, whole and ground oats are used in place of white flour and combined with pecans, brown sugar, and spices for a tantalizing topping that would be delicious draped over nearly anything—think berries, peaches, or pears. SERVES 4 TO 6

5 tablespoons unsalted butter, divided, plus more for greasing

1 cup old-fashioned rolled oats (regular or gluten-free), divided

¼ cup plus 3 tablespoons packed light brown sugar, divided

½ teaspoon ground cinnamon, divided

Pinch freshly ground nutmeg

⅛ teaspoon kosher salt

⅓ cup pecans

5 medium Granny Smith apples (about 2 pounds), peeled, cored, and cut into 1-inch dice

Whipped cream or vanilla ice cream, for serving (optional)

1. Preheat the oven to 375°F. Butter an 8-by-8-inch or similar size baking dish.

2. Fit the mini food processor with the *s blade*. Add ½ cup of oats, and process to the texture of coarse flour.

3. Add ¼ cup of brown sugar, ¼ teaspoon of cinnamon, the nutmeg, and salt. Process to combine.

4. Add the pecans, and pulse until coarsely chopped, about 6 pulses. Add the remaining ½ cup of oats, and pulse twice to combine.

5. Melt 4 tablespoons of butter, and pour it over the mixture in the processor. Pulse until the butter is distributed and the mixture looks damp, about 10 pulses.

6. Toss the apples with the remaining 3 tablespoons of brown sugar and ¼ teaspoon of cinnamon. Transfer to the baking dish. Cut the remaining tablespoon of butter into small pieces, and dot it over the apples. Sprinkle the crisp topping evenly on top.

7. Cover the crisp tightly with foil, and bake for 35 minutes. Remove the foil, and bake for 30 minutes longer, or until the top is browned and the apples are tender. Let cool slightly.

8. Serve warm or at room temperature, with a dollop of whipped cream or ice cream, if you wish.

STORAGE Leftovers can be stored at room temperature or in the refrigerator for up to 2 days. It makes for a great breakfast!

Pumpkin Pie

Prep time: 30 minutes, plus 30 minutes to cool
Cook time: 1 hour, 15 minutes

NUT-FREE, VEGETARIAN

I know everybody uses the recipe from the back of the pumpkin purée can. It's what I grew up with, and it's delicious. But if I can pry you away, this version is worth it. The texture is velvety and smooth, thanks to the food processor, and the filling comes together in just 10 minutes. The pie is baked low and slow, ensuring a silky-smooth custard. It gets extra depth of flavor from a touch of brandy or dark rum as well as brown sugar—two tricks I learned from Elisabeth Prueitt in her book Tartine. MAKES 1 (9-INCH) PIE

FOR THE CRUST

All-purpose flour, for flouring

½ recipe Classic Pie Dough (page 77)

FOR THE PIE

1½ cups homemade pumpkin purée or
    canned pumpkin

2 eggs

¾ cup heavy (whipping) cream

1 tablespoon brandy or dark rum

⅓ cup packed light brown sugar

1 teaspoon ground cinnamon

½ teaspoon ground ginger

⅛ teaspoon ground cloves

⅛ teaspoon freshly grated nutmeg

½ teaspoon kosher salt

Whipped cream, for serving

STORAGE You can make the crust the day before; cover it with plastic wrap, and store it at room temperature.

TO MAKE THE CRUST

1. Preheat the oven to 425°F.

2. Lightly flour a work surface, and roll out the dough into an ⅛-thick round. Transfer the dough to a 9-inch pie plate, pressing it into the corners. Trim the edge, leaving a half-inch overhang. Roll the overhang underneath itself to form a rim. Crimp or flute as desired. Line the dough with parchment paper, and fill it with dried beans or pie weights, making sure to get into the edges. Bake until light golden, 10 to 15 minutes.

3. Remove the parchment and weights. Reduce the temperature to 375°F, and bake for 5 to 7 minutes longer, or until golden on the bottom.

4. Let cool completely on a rack.

TO MAKE THE PIE

1. Preheat the oven to 325°F.

2. Fit the food processor with the *s blade*. Add the pumpkin, eggs, heavy cream, brandy, brown sugar, cinnamon, ginger, cloves, nutmeg, and salt, and process until smooth.

3. Pour the filling into the prebaked pie crust. Bake for 55 to 65 minutes, or until the filling is set but still wobbles slightly in the middle when jiggled.

4. Cool the pie on a wire rack, and serve with whipped cream.

STORAGE The pumpkin pie can be refrigerated for up to 4 days.

HOW-TO To make your own pumpkin purée, halve a sugar pumpkin, and scrape out the seeds. Bake the pumpkin, cut-side down, on a lightly oiled, parchment-lined baking sheet in a 375°F oven until tender, 40 to 50 minutes. Scoop the flesh into a food processor fitted with the *s blade*. Process until smooth, stopping and scraping down the sides occasionally—this will take several minutes. Work the pumpkin through a strainer with a spatula, pressing and scraping—this will ensure a completely smooth purée. One sugar pumpkin yields about 2 cups of purée.

Two-Layer Carrot Cake

Prep time: 45 minutes, plus 30 minutes to chill and 10 minutes to soak

Cook time: 40 minutes

VEGETARIAN

I don't know if it's the moist and dense texture, the mix of warming spices, or the tangy cream cheese frosting, but carrot cake is the one cake I'll take over pie. However, it's not the quickest cake to make, involving several steps and numerous mixing bowls. Food processor to the rescue! Using the processor to shred the carrots and then to blend the wet ingredients (with no washing in between), the procedure is streamlined, requiring only 1 mixing bowl. The processor also produces the smoothest, creamiest cream cheese frosting ever, in only minutes. MAKES 1 CAKE

FOR THE CAKE

Butter, for greasing

½ cup currants

2¼ cups all-purpose flour

1 teaspoon baking powder

1 teaspoon baking soda

¾ teaspoon kosher salt

1½ teaspoons ground cinnamon

¼ teaspoon ground nutmeg

¼ teaspoon ground allspice

½ cup chopped pecans

8 medium carrots (about 1 pound), trimmed and peeled

4 eggs

1 cup packed light brown sugar

1 cup granulated sugar

2 teaspoons vanilla extract

1 cup grapeseed or canola oil

FOR THE FROSTING

2 (8-ounce) packages cream cheese, at room temperature

12 tablespoons unsalted butter, at room temperature

1 tablespoon vanilla extract

1 cup confectioners' sugar

TO MAKE THE CAKE

1. Preheat the oven to 375°F. Butter 2 (9-inch) cake pans, and line the bottoms with parchment paper rounds.

2. Cover the currants with hot water, and let soak for 10 minutes. Drain and set aside.

3. In a large bowl, whisk together the flour, baking powder, baking soda, salt, cinnamon, nutmeg, and allspice. Stir in the pecans.

4. Fit the food processor with the *shredding disc*. Push the carrots through the feed tube to shred. Transfer to the bowl with the flour, and stir to combine.

5. Refit the processor with the *s blade* (no need to wash). Add the eggs, brown sugar, granulated sugar, and vanilla, and process until smooth. With the motor running, slowly drizzle the grapeseed oil through the feed tube, and process until combined.

6. Pour the wet ingredients over the dry ingredients in the bowl, and stir with a rubber spatula until combined. Add the currants, and fold to combine.

7. Divide the batter between the 2 cake pans, smoothing the tops. Bake until the cakes are browned and a toothpick inserted in the center comes out clean, 30 to 40 minutes. Transfer to a wire rack, and cool for 5 minutes. Run a knife along the edge of the pans, then invert the pans to remove the cakes. Peel off and discard the parchment. Turn the cakes over so that they're right-side up. Cool completely on the wire rack.

STORAGE The unfrosted cakes can be wrapped in double layers of plastic wrap and refrigerated for up to 2 days. Once frosted, the cake can be covered with a dome or large bowl and refrigerated for up to 1 day.

TO MAKE THE FROSTING

1. Fit the food processor with the *s blade*. Add the cream cheese and butter, and process until smooth, stopping and scraping down the sides occasionally. Add the vanilla, and process to incorporate. Stop and scrape down the sides.

2. Add ½ cup of the sugar, and process until smooth. Add the remaining ½ cup of sugar, and process until the frosting is completely smooth, stopping and scraping down the sides occasionally.

3. When the cakes are completely cool, place one layer on a cake stand or large plate. Cover the top with frosting (if the frosting is too soft to work with, put it in the refrigerator for a few minutes to firm up). Place the second cake on top, flat-side (bottom) up. Spread the remaining frosting over the top and sides of the cake. If needed, refrigerate the cake for at least 30 minutes before serving, to allow the frosting to set. Slice and serve.

Menus for Special Occasions

One of my favorite things about entertaining is planning the menu—curling up with a notebook and a pile of recipes and deciding which dishes to make. Pour me a glass of wine, and I'm in heaven. I've been told, however, that not everybody enjoys this process. (A good friend recently likened menu planning to doing her own taxes—eek!) I therefore thought I'd save you the trouble and share some of my favorite menus for special occasions, all featuring dishes right from this book. From holiday dinners to birthday parties and football games, I've got you covered. Happy cooking!

Holiday Meal

Birthday Celebration

Baby or Wedding Shower Brunch

Fourth of July or Summer Party

Super Bowl or Football Game

The Dirty Dozen &
The Clean Fifteen

A nonprofit and environmental watchdog organization called Environmental Working Group (EWG) looks at data supplied by the US Department of Agriculture (USDA) and the Food and Drug Administration (FDA) about pesticide residues and compiles a list each year of the best and worst pesticide loads found in commercial crops. You can refer to the Dirty Dozen list to know which fruits and vegetables you should always buy organic. The Clean Fifteen list lets you know which produce is considered safe enough when grown conventionally to allow you to skip the organics. This does not mean that the Clean Fifteen produce is pesticide-free, though, so wash these fruits and vegetables thoroughly. These lists change every year, so make sure you look up the most recent before you fill your shopping cart. You'll find the most recent lists as well as a guide to pesticides in produce at EWG.org/FoodNews.

Dirty Dozen

APPLES
CELERY
CHERRY TOMATOES
CUCUMBERS
GRAPES
NECTARINES
PEACHES
POTATOES
SNAP PEAS
SPINACH
STRAWBERRIES
SWEET BELL PEPPERS

In addition to the Dirty Dozen, the EWG added two foods contaminated with highly toxic organophosphate insecticides:

HOT PEPPERS
KALE/COLLARD GREENS

Clean Fifteen

ASPARAGUS
AVOCADOS
CABBAGE
CANTALOUPE
CAULIFLOWER
EGGPLANT
GRAPEFRUIT
KIWIS
MANGOS
ONIONS
PAPAYAS
PINEAPPLES
SWEET CORN
SWEET PEAS (FROZEN)
SWEET POTATOES

Measurement Conversions

Volume Equivalents (Liquid)

US STANDARD	US STANDARD (OUNCES)	METRIC (APPROXIMATE)
2 tablespoons	1 fl. oz.	30 mL
¼ cup	2 fl. oz.	60 mL
½ cup	4 fl. oz.	120 mL
1 cup	8 fl. oz.	240 mL
1½ cups	12 fl. oz.	355 mL
2 cups or 1 pint	16 fl. oz.	475 mL
4 cups or 1 quart	32 fl. oz.	1 L
1 gallon	128 fl. oz.	4 L

Oven Temperatures

FAHRENHEIT (F)	CELSIUS (C) (APPROXIMATE)
250°F	120°C
300°F	150°C
325°F	165°C
350°F	180°C
375°F	190°C
400°F	200°C
425°F	220°C
450°F	230°C

Volume Equivalents (Dry)

US STANDARD	METRIC (APPROXIMATE)
⅛ teaspoon	0.5 mL
¼ teaspoon	1 mL
½ teaspoon	2 mL
¾ teaspoon	4 mL
1 teaspoon	5 mL
1 tablespoon	15 mL
¼ cup	59 mL
⅓ cup	79 mL
½ cup	118 mL
⅔ cup	156 mL
¾ cup	177 mL
1 cup	235 mL
2 cups or 1 pint	475 mL
3 cups	700 mL
4 cups or 1 quart	1 L

Weight Equivalents

US STANDARD	METRIC (APPROXIMATE)
½ ounce	15 g
1 ounce	30 g
2 ounces	60 g
4 ounces	115 g
8 ounces	225 g
12 ounces	340 g
16 ounces or 1 pound	455 g

Recipe Index

Index

Acknowledgments

Thank you to James, for inspiring me to follow my passion, for encouraging me to stick with it, and, of course, for being the ultimate partner and taste tester. I love you to Pluto and back (and then some).

Thank you to Ella and Juniper, who have taught me that in moments of intense stress, it's best to have an epic dance party. Let's keep on dancing, girls.

Thank you to my editor, Stacy, who found me, believed in me, and cheered me on from day one.

Thank you to my mom, who swooped in like Mary Poppins to help when we needed it most and who amazes me with her limitless joy and selflessness. Thank you to my dad, who taught me how to work hard to achieve my dreams and who has always been such a solid rock in our lives.

Thank you to Caroline for bringing my recipes to life through your beautiful photographs, and to my SWAT team—Amanda, Kelley, Heather, and Ana—for your incredible support and help in getting this book out the door. Love you, ladies.

Thank you to my friends and mentors near and far. I'm so grateful to have such amazing people in my life who continually inspire and ground me. You know who you are.

And thank you to my readers, who are committed to cooking fresh foods from scratch for themselves and their families, even though it isn't always easy. I'll always have your back.

About the Author

Nicki Sizemore is a recipe developer, food stylist, video host, and cooking instructor with over a decade of experience in the food industry. She has worked with publications including *Taste of Home* and *Fine Cooking*, among others, and she is the author of the blog *From Scratch Fast*, featuring dishes that can be made from scratch in under an hour. She lives in the Hudson Valley, New York, with her husband and two daughters.

Follow Nicki online

www.nickisizemore.com/blog

@SizemoreNicki

f facebook.com/FromScratchFast

CPSIA information can be obtained
at www.ICGtesting.com
Printed in the USA
LVOW05s1524161215

466846LV00001B/1/P